More of Len's Stories

By

Len Holder
Master Mariner

Dedication:
To Ann for her dedication and support

First Published 2010 by Appin Press, an imprint of Countyvise Ltd
14 Appin Road, Birkenhead, CH41 9HH

British Library Cataloguing in Publication Data.
A catalogue record for this book is available from the British Library.

ISBN 978 1 906205 52 2

Introduction

The Author

My first book of stories "A Light-Hearted Look at Seafaring and other stories" has opened up a number of new avenues. Many of the people I wrote about have been in touch, appreciating the stories and so far nobody has wanted to punch me on the nose. Many who read the book have written from the four corners of the globe and told me their own stories.

I have been invited to give talks to Probus, Rotary and Lions Clubs, Women's Institutes (a bit scary) and Guilds and village community groups. We have shared our experiences and observations of human nature and life.

When I put the first book "to bed", my mind kept recalling other stories and life around me continued to present amusing incidents, stories worth telling, so here are some more of the same, or similar stories. I hope you enjoy them.

The charities that have benefited from the proceeds of the book have used the money well, so we will continue to use the income from this second book to support maritime and medical charities in the same way.

Foreword
by the Reverend Canon Bob Evans MBE BA RNR

Len Holder is known and respected throughout the maritime industry, not only in this country, but worldwide. The reason is quite simple. He understands what makes a seafarer tick.

But there is more to it than that. He is a natural communicator. It was many decades ago that I first met him and Ann and the delightful family. I was Chaplain Superintendent of the Mersey Mission to Seamen for almost thirty years and Len quickly won the hearts of all of us. You could not avoid Len Holder! He was Head of Maritime Studies at Liverpool Polytechnic and went on to expand the educational field on a worldwide basis. His influence and contribution to the seafaring world is not to be underestimated and it is reflected in these memoirs.

His first book was enthralling and this one promises to surpass it. It is all about people… mostly seafaring folk… and it is full of fun. I think the first task of a communicator is to make you smile and pay attention. This book does just that.

A Foreword is only to be glanced at….read the book.

Contents

3   More Seafaring Stories

6 More Holidays and Travel

7   More Cultural Exchanges

8 More Home and Family

The Story Continues

1. Digital Photographic Techniques

Looking for a cover picture for the first "Light-Hearted Look" book, we found an appropriate picture that Ann had taken on board the sailing barge "Kitty" in the Solent.

The only problem was that the picture contained a strange woman – not THAT sort of strange, just someone we did not know.

Easy, I thought, we can airbrush her out and put Ann in the picture instead. Not being an expert at "doctoring" photographs, I captured a picture of Ann's head from elsewhere and stuck it on the woman. I did not get it quite right!

As you will see from the illustration, it looked very odd.

Nothing for it but to re-brush the area with sea. Ann appeared on the title page instead. Lesson learned – manipulating digital images is more difficult than I thought!

2. A Japanese Perspective

The book cover picture went down very well in Japan. The first person to buy a book, Mr Hirotaka Shirota wrote: "Thank you for your book. I am pleased to have received wonderful book today. Captain Len on cover page look like Hollywood Star and Japanese Cherry Blossom's picture on 170 page is nice."

Another Japanese friend Mr Motohei Kobayashi was reading the book at home in the New Year holidays. His daughter, home from University, noticed the cover picture and asked if her father was reading about pirates. He told her: "No! It is about my friend Captain Len!" She said she thought it was about Captain Jack Sparrow (played by Johnny Depp) from Pirates of the Caribbean.
I had never been mistaken for a film star before!

Captain Sparrow   *"Captain Len"*

3.   A Safety Message from the Author:

My family had a phone call yesterday from one of my former shipmates from 50+ years ago - a retired ship master. He received a copy of my book in the post yesterday morning and thought he would read a couple of stories. He got engrossed in the book and read it from cover to cover - forgetting he was cooking cakes for visiting (grand) children. Meanwhile the cakes were incinerated in the kitchen. A new version of the King Alfred story - perhaps I should include a safety warning with each copy? Earlier in his life he had forgotten what was cooking and burned a new £8,000 kitchen.

**For those who have forgotten:
English King Alfred's Story**.

By 870 the Danes had overthrown the kingdoms of East Anglia, Northumbria, and Mercia, and were preparing to do the same to Wessex. Standing in their way was a young king of Wessex, Alfred by name. At first the fight went badly for Alfred; some of his allies found it more expedient to cooperate with the Danes, and in 877 he was pushed back to a small corner of the marshes around Athelney, in Somerset.

Statue of King Alfred

The tale of the griddle-cakes. It is this time, at the low ebb of Anglo Saxon resistance to the Danes, that is commemorated in the folk tale of Alfred and the griddle cakes. The story goes that Alfred was so low in his fortunes that he was forced to travel anonymously and seek lodging in a peasant woman's hut. Told to mind the cakes cooking on the fire, Alfred let his thoughts wander to his troubles. The cakes burned, and the peasant woman gave her king a good scolding for his carelessness. True or not, (probably not, but it sounds good), the story illustrates the depth to which the young Alfred had sunk in his battle with the Danish invaders. From that point on, however, things began to look up, as anyone who has seen his statue in Winchester will know…

Back To The Early Days

1. Brothers and Sisters

Having a brother five years younger than yourself and a sister about five years older, was not always easy, especially when it came to the odd rough and tumble fights. I was defenceless: you cannot hit girls and you cannot hit people younger than yourself.

Len, Robin and Elizabeth

During World War II the family had a big Cossor battery radio on which we listened to broadcasts about the war on the BBC Home Service. The radio had a tall wooden case with a cloth-covered speaker at the bottom and a glass tuning dial at the top with the stations and wavelengths marked on it.

On one occasion brother Robin aged about 3 or 4, picked up a marble and threw it at me with all the force he could muster. I saw it coming, ducked, and the marble shattered the tuning dial. For the rest of the war we managed with a few pencil marks under the pointer.

The injustice is that he was not told off for throwing the marble, I was reprimanded for ducking!

2. Every Sea Scout

My sister Elizabeth recently reminded me about a misunderstanding that arose when our younger brother Robin joined the 4th Dovercourt Sea Scouts. I should explain that Harwich is the main East Coast Depot for Trinity House, the organisation that looks after buoys, lightships and navigation marks around the coast. Trinity House had several ships operating out of Harwich, T.H.V.s Patricia, Ready, Alert and Triton, being regulars at the Trinity House pier.

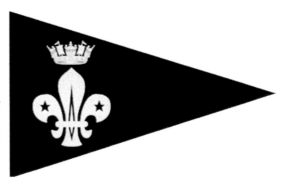

The Admiralty Pennant, displayed by recognised Sea Scout Groups such as the 4th Dovercourt

Robin came home from one of his first scout meetings and announced to the family that he had to go aboard one of the Trinity House ships. We were a bit surprised until we discovered that the scoutmaster had told him "Every sea scout has to be on the alert!" I think he was a bit disappointed that it did not involve going on a ship.

3. Action and Reaction

We were taught at school about the laws of physics. Newton's Third Law states that forces occur in pairs, one called the Action and the other the Reaction (actio et reactio in latin). To every Action, there is an equal and opposite Reaction.

A demonstration of this occurred at the Halfpenny Pier at Harwich when we had been sailing and brought the dinghy into the steps. The bow was against the steps and the first two ashore carried some of the gear (oars, lifejackets, anchor, sails, spare ropes, bailer etc) up the steps and onto the pier. Danny Goswell who was in charge of operations, was in the stern and collected another armful of gear. Unfortunately the first two ashore had had their hands full and had not tied the bowline to the steps. Danny started to walk forward and, as Newton dictated, the boat started to move astern. Realising the gap was widening, Danny went faster, and as Newton dictated, so did the boat. As he reached the bow, he was moving so fast he could not stop and stepped straight into the water. The two of us who were first ashore had a good laugh but had to suffer Danny's wrath for a few days!

The Halfpenny Pier at Harwich (no steps now)

Scout Boat "Venturer"

18

4. Sailing Clubs and Yacht Clubs

When I first learned to sail, my friends told me that there are two types of club associated with sailing. The one where we were based, Harwich and Dovercourt Sailing Club was very friendly. If members saw anyone struggling to get their boat out of the water or stuck in the mud of Patrick's Creek, they would all gather round and help.

The old concrete barge: HQ of Harwich and Dovercourt Sailing Club (now in Gashouse Creek)

The first time we arrived at the landing stage of the Royal Harwich Yacht Club at Woolverstone in the Sea Scout's boat full of camping gear, we discovered it was the other sort of club. It was early evening and the members stood outside the clubhouse in their smart blazers, gins and tonics in hand and politely discussed our plight – but nobody offered to help. If we ever got into trouble, we knew what to expect.

19

"Venturer" off the Royal Harwich Yacht Club at Woolverstone

A couple of years later, I had borrowed a 27-foot sailing whaler from the Royal Navy's reserve fleet. We moored the boat at the Halfpenny pier at Harwich overnight and were keen to catch the tide up the River Orwell next morning. The pier was busy and we could only get the bow of the boat up to the steps. We dumped all the spare gear, sails, ropes, anchor etc in the bow and set off. There was a brisk northerly blowing as we came level with the Royal Harwich in mid afternoon. For two people, the whaler was a bit of a handful. As we careered rapidly towards the neat row of moored smart Royal Harwich yachts, I sent the crew forward to clear one of the ropes. I should not have done that, because the rudder came out of the water and we could not turn.

I looked ahead in horror and saw that the after cockpit of the yacht we were approaching had a table laid out for afternoon tea, and two well-dressed couples were sipping from the best china cups.

As we hurtled towards them I sensed impending disaster, but when we were a few feet off, one of the gentlemen leaned down in the cockpit and brought out a beautiful, neat circular fender which he hung over the side of their boat. Our sharp bow hit the fender, the cups rattled a bit, their boat was pushed round in a complete circle and we sailed away on the other tack. They were very polite. No expletives were used. They just said "Good Afternoon!" as the boats locked together and then came apart.

5. Walton Backwaters

Aged 13 or 14, our year's sailing in the 12ft "Osprey" started with voyages of exploration in the rivers Stour and Orwell: Levington Creek, Pin Mill, Woolverstone, Wrabness, Holbrook etc. Several people suggested that a very good day's sailing was out of Harwich Harbour and across Dovercourt Bay to Walton Backwaters, where there were miles of creeks to be explored. We decided to give it a try. Danny Goswell, as skipper, did his homework. We would nip round the stone breakwater at low tide and the flood tide would carry us across the bay and into the Backwaters.

On the chosen day, the only problem was the wind – a bit too much of it to be comfortable. We had arranged to sail in company with Brian Waters, the Harbour Master's son, who had a 14-foot dinghy. Our first stop was the beach at Dovercourt, where Brian picked up Clive Reynolds as extra crew. We sailed out into the bay, Danny at the helm, me with a bucket, past the Pye End Buoy (nearly through the Pye End buoy because we were busy sailing and baling and did not see it). Each wave we hit came straight over the bow (we had no foredeck) and half flooded the boat. Then we turned towards the south and had a clear run into the backwaters. We lost contact with the other boat. We had a great day exploring the twists and turns of the creeks. At one point we wanted to get across towards Walton on the Naze. We just could not find a gap in the bank to get across into the next creek, so we decided to sail across the mud. We took up the centreboard, ran before the wind, both sitting in the stern, rose up onto the bank on a large wave, I rushed to the bow, the stern rose up and we slid in and sailed away towards Walton. Who needs sand yachts!

When the tide started to ebb, we decided to leave, so as not to be left high and dry. We crept back along the shore across Dovercourt Bay with the tidal stream carrying us northwards.

We passed very close to the end of the Stone Breakwater and made our way in to Harwich Pier against a strong ebb tide. Brian "Wet" Waters had not done his homework, he sailed across towards Felixstowe and got caught on the ebb tide. We last saw them disappearing into the North Sea over the horizon. It was a good job Brian's father was a man of influence – he persuaded the British Rail ferry "Brightlingsea" to go out to sea and tow them in.

As I made my way home in the dark, I met my father coming to look for me. We had had a wonderful exhilarating adventure. Thank goodness our parents did not know the risks we were taking!

6. Thames Barges

I wanted to sail in a Thames Barge and at the age of 16, I asked F T Everards of Greenhithe Kent for a summer holiday trip. They would not let me sail in the "Cambria" which they kept for racing as a pure-sail craft. They said the skipper was a real old misery and very hard-case, but good at winning barge races. They arranged for me to sail for six weeks in the "Will Everard" with Captain Uglow as skipper. Much to my disappointment there was a dock strike for the whole six weeks. The barge was trapped in London Docks, so my trip was called off. Many years later, completely out of the blue, our middle son Nicholas, who worked for IBM in Portsmouth, booked

Thames Barge off Parkeston

a Father's Day treat for Ann and I on the "Kitty", which sails out of Port Solent.

"Kitty" was built in 1895, one of 37 barges built by J & H Cann at Gas House Creek, Harwich. Cann's were renowned for both high quality workmanship and a reputation for building fast vessels. This reputation for speed is evidenced by the number of East Coast Barge races she has won over the years. Doing 10.4 knots under full sail with the tide behind us was exhilarating. Steering the barge was very easy – the sails and hull are in such harmony that they almost sail themselves.

The skipper told us a story about a barge that did sail itself. "Lady Daphne" was known as the "lucky Lady Daphne" for an extraordinary incident. On Boxing Day 1927, the skipper jumped overboard to rescue the boy, who had fallen in off the Cornish coast, and could not swim. "Lady Daphne", `guided´ by the skipper's canary, sailed herself through the rocks of the Scilly Isles onto a few tens of yards of safe sand in St Mary's Harbour. It sounded like an old sea dog's tale. A few days later I recounted the tale amongst a group of experienced seafarers making a Videotel training video on "Search and Rescue". One of our number said he could confirm the story. As a boy he used to spend holidays in St Mary's with his uncle who was the local Coastguard Officer. He had actually seen the Lady Daphne sail into the harbour and when she went aground on the sand, obviously abandoned, rowed his single handed dinghy across the harbour to claim "salvage". The crew of a very fast six-oared racing pilot gig beat him to it!

7. Career Choices: Why Did I Go To Sea?

I have always been interested to find out whether or not people leaving school made the right career choice and if so, what influenced them in making their choice. Retirement has made me look back at my own choice and to think how and why I made it.

Where We Lived

The picture of haymaking shows both my grandfathers and other family members. Being brought up in a tiny hamlet in the Weald of Sussex, surrounded by farmland, in a house with no gas or electricity, I should logically have become an agricultural worker like most of the other boys in the village, but from the earliest days boats fascinated me. My father had a shed (a workshop, a vice and a coping saw) and I used to make very small wooden battleships and aircraft carriers. They had to be small because my test tank was the water butt next to the shed.

I remember my aircraft carriers all capsized because the bridge structure was on one side. I put a metal "keel" under the port side. They no longer capsized – they just sank! I had to add more buoyancy by making the hull deeper.

Then they floated upright! My first practical lessons in ship stability! Later in life I went on to fail at first attempt the highly mathematical Naval Architecture paper in the Extra Master's Examination. Perhaps I am better at trial and error than pure theory.

I soon found the water butt rather limiting, and dammed the ditch (stream) that ran past the back of the house. At the age of 12 we moved to the seaside in Dovercourt Bay, Essex and more opportunities to get involved with boats.

Family: Parents

My father, Sergeant Arthur Holder RASC, served in Salonika in the First World War in transport (mainly with mules and horses) and was fascinated by motorcycles, cars and vans. He spent the happiest days of his life in jobs that involved a lot of driving. My mother loved children and, giving up the opportunity for a scholarship to grammar school to help with family finances, became a children's nurse. As a young teenager, she was nurse to the youngest child, David Naismith,  son of the Captain Superintendent at Dartmouth Royal Naval College. Smart young Royal Naval officers impressed her. Was it through her influence that I found myself applying for entry into Dartmouth Royal Naval College?

Family: A Favourite Uncle

My mother's brother, Leonard Arthur Hatcher (after whom I was named) wrote to me regularly during my school days. The family were proud of his achievements. From an unimpressive educational start at a local Board School in Deptford in London, he had transferred to London Nautical School in Rotherhithe, gone to sea and obtained his Master Mariner's Certificate and served at sea as a senior officer in World War II. After the war he became a Harbour Master in Malaya. He sent me stamps for my stamp collection. He arranged for me to write to a Chinese Malay boy of about my own age, Lim Chin Seng. Whilst Uncle Len was on vacation with us in Sussex, I took

Uncle 'Leonard Arthur Hatcher'

him fishing with me. He, and his wife Winifred, were very smartly dressed. While he borrowed the rod and tried his hand, I leaned forward on the net and fell in. I could not swim but managed to "doggy paddle" to the bank. Soaked to the skin, I wore Aunty Win's best fur coat on the long walk home.

He was a bit of a role model for me. From Malaya, he sent £100 for me to buy my kit when I went to sea. On my second voyage I met him in Penang. We went to a cocktail

27

party. Having had a couple of drinks he surprised me by saying: "Why did you go to sea? It is a lousy life, away from your family and friends." I said "Hang on a minute, for years you have been supporting me in going to sea!" He replied "Several years ago your mother wrote and said she thought you wanted to go to sea, and she was not happy about it. I told her that the best way was not to oppose the idea, which would make you more determined. Just say nothing and you would change your mind. You didn't! You let me down!" I had missed his hidden agenda, but still enjoyed my years at sea.

The Influence of the Cinema and Books

I enjoyed films like "The Cruel Sea" and other naval epics. It all looked very exciting. I read books about ships, like "The Wheel's Kick and the Wind's Song" by Captain A G Course and "The Cruel Sea" by Nicholas Monsarrat.

Very recently I gave a talk about my career choices. Afterwards a retired gentleman approached me and said: "When I left school, I wanted to be a gamekeeper, but my headmaster said it was an unsuitable career for a grammar school boy. The headmaster asked me 'What did your father do?' I told him that my father was in the Civil Service. The headmaster thought that was a respectable career."
I asked what choice he eventually made.
He said "I joined the Civil Service."
So he did not choose, his headmaster did!
About the time he and I left school there was a big court case about "Lady Chatterley's Lover" by D H Lawrence. I wonder: "Had he read it before he decided to choose gamekeeping?"

School Teachers

Several of the men who joined the Harwich County High School staff after the war had been in the Royal Air Force, so if we had taken them as role models, we would have all been flying. For some strange reason, only the girls were allowed to do Biology, with one exception, Danny Goswell, who as well as being interested in girls, wanted to be a vet. Whether this rule was to keep the boys in total ignorance or because the Headmaster thought they knew enough already, was never made clear. It messed up my chances for Dartmouth because the option papers were General Science or Latin. Without Biology I might have struggled with General Science, so I concentrated on Latin. It is good to know that half of the officers patrolling the world to protect us know the declension of amo, amas, amat etc The Latin Class had Virgil's Aeneid as set book in the GCE Examinations. I was not bad at translation and used to sell my version to all the boys in the back row at sixpence a time. This worked well as my book was passed along under the desks, until one desk was moved across a wide gangway. We thought Mr Thompson did not know, but after a long wait he said "For goodness sake pass Holder's book across and let us get on with the lesson!" Anyway, I passed Latin in the Royal Naval Entry exam.

Sea Scouts and Meeting People

Before moving to the Essex coast, we had holidays staying in Dovercourt with my grandparents. I had enjoyed seeing the ships and rowing and canoeing on the boating lake. When we moved, I talked to the other boys in the 3rd year about learning to sail. They said I should join the 4th Dovercourt Sea Scouts, which I did. They were a great bunch and I enjoyed the activities especially rowing and sailing in the scout boat "Venturer" and in whalers borrowed from the reserve fleet. Older boys who had already left and joined the Merchant Navy came to see us. One in particular was Graham Kemp Lucke. He showed us how tough he was by allowing us each in turn to punch his stomach with no visible effects! They regaled us with stories of their voyages and adventures. Another influence on my choice of careers.

Careers Masters and Careers Advisers
Later in life, when I was in the in Wirral Choral Society, I stood next to a bass whose day job was as a Careers Master. He said he had two pupils who were very keen to go to sea. He said "They were so keen! It took me weeks to persuade them that the Merchant Navy was a dying industry and there was no future in careers at sea." This was at a time when the British Shipping Careers service was actively trying to find enough youngsters to fill the available training berths and officer positions on our ships. Definitely a case of crossed wires.

The Careers Masters who really depressed me were the ones with a little book in which it said:

With one "O" level you can do job X, with two "O" levels you can do Y, etc right up to the opportunities which needed four or five "A" levels. Although this is a realistic starting point for career choice, there is a lot more to job satisfaction than relying on the number of examinations you pass. Personal interests, practical aptitudes, family and social factors should all play a part. I even met young people who had been told that, if they had four "O" levels, it would be a waste of their opportunities to consider any jobs that needed only 2 or 3. I despaired.

The Merchant Navy had both "O" and "A" Level cadet entry routes and were always fighting against parents and headmasters who saw only the academic ways ahead, to the Sixth Form and University, respectively. What a difference when we started an entry route for University Graduates where University Careers Advisers really wanted to make sure people got into the right jobs, which used their talents and made them happy.

My overall conclusions on career choices are that, no matter how much research they do, no young person knows all the facts about opportunities and pitfalls and they are lucky if they choose correctly. I really admire those brave young people who, having made their choice, realise it was wrong and start again. Sadly, many carry on in work they do not enjoy.

8. The Great London Smog of December 1952

With industries and many homes in London burning coal or wood for fuel, pollution levels were very high in London and this was compounded when high pressure and an inversion was present trapping pollution near the surface. This is what happened in December 1952.

I was attending a pre-sea three-month course at King Edward VII Nautical College in Stepney, in the East End of London and living with my Uncle George and Aunty Dorothy Packer at the London Fire Brigade Headquarters on Albert Embankment opposite, and just up-river from, the Houses of Parliament.

High pressure was over the UK during the early part of December 1952 and dense fog formed in the calm conditions. Sulphur dioxide produced by coal burning attracts water molecules and produces a fine spray of sulphurous and sulphuric acid. The effect of this increases the density of the fog, visibility can be as low as a few metres and gives it a yellow tinge, the pea-souper.

Public transport stopped and the only way to get about was on foot. I recall walking down Whitehall in late afternoon and not being able to see my feet on the pavement. Several times I stepped off the obscured pavement and nearly fell, after which I decided to walk in the roadway in the eerie silence.

It is believed that the smog of early December 1952 may have claimed the lives of 4000 people although the

Guinness Book of Records has it at 2850, some even put the figure as high as 12,000.

I walked over Lambeth Bridge and was within a few yards of the Fire Brigade HQ when I came across a car crawling through the fog. The driver called to me and said "This is hopeless. Is there anywhere nearby where that I can park safely and walk?" We were on the southern approach to the bridge, and just opposite was the Archbishop of Canterbury's Lambeth Palace, with plenty of parking space outside. I indicated the direction to him and he drove slowly away into the fog. I walked off in the opposite direction. In a few minutes I heard an ominous crashing and scraping of metal.

If you have ever seen the film "Genevieve" about the London to Brighton "Old Crocks" Race, you may remember the old car coming across Lambeth Bridge and getting its narrow wheels caught in the tram tracks, which veered it off course. I had forgotten that the tram tracks were being removed at that time and the poor man had driven into the roadworks. Oops! I felt very sorry!

A couple of years later, I was on a Glen Line ship in the Royal Docks in London, when the sky went black and we had complete darkness at 3 pm in the afternoon during another foggy day. The 1956 Clean Air Act eventually stopped the London smogs. In the 1800s London was nearly brought to a standstill with mounds of horse manure from the transport. In the 21st century we just have exhaust fumes.

9. Taking "Venturer" to Flatford Mill

In the mid 1950s two intrepid 4th Dovercourt Sea Scouts, Peter Wright and Len Holder, decided to undertake an "epic" voyage to the historic and world-renowned Flatford Mill of John Constable fame. The scout boat "Venturer" was very robust and heavy (an old lightship's lifeboat) and it was not going to be easy.

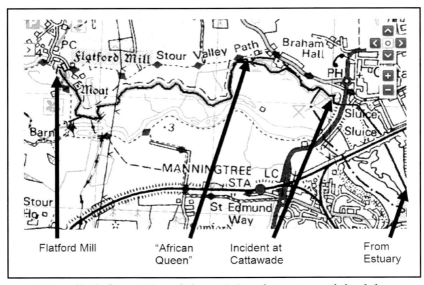

Flatford Mill　　　"African　　Incident at　　From
　　　　　　　　　Queen"　　Cattawade　　Estuary

We sailed from Harwich to Manningtree and had been advised that when the river split into two channels, we should take the northern branch as the wider southern channel was very shallow. As far as we know, apart from odd canoes that could haul out and bypass difficult parts, no-one had taken a boat up to Flatford since before World War 2. Thus, it gave a resident of a houseboat at Cattawade quite a surprise as she sunbathed in the nude by the river,

34

when the rushes and reeds parted and we appeared. Surprised at first, she ran for cover and reappeared fully clothed to offer us hospitality and a tour of her home, of which she was very proud.

Moving on, we passed Brantham Mill, which Peter remembers as being a wonderful old spice mill with its machinery polished with age. Past the mill there was a lock to negotiate and the water was really shallow. We had the sails up, but the scene was very reminiscent to the adventures of Humphrey Bogart and Katherine Hepburn in the film "African Queen" – get out and walk!

Further up river the water was deeper and we were able to ask a group of Friars, walking on the towpath, whether we were on the right route and how far it was to the mill.

Eventually we arrived at the mill – quite an achievement. We slept in the boat but it was not very restful, with the water cascading noisily over the weir under the mill.

The next day we tried to get through the lock to

go further up-river to Dedham, but despite Peter bravely entering the lock chamber and levering the sluices with oars, the lock had not been opened for years and would not budge. We were not going to get any further.

Nevertheless it gave us a great deal of satisfaction to have made it that far up the river in a big heavy boat.

10. Overcoats

I had joined a shipping company that traded to Australia and the Far East and I did not often need an overcoat. When my uncle sent £100 for me to buy my uniform, the outfitters had talked me into paying a large part of it for a rather splendid navy blue tailored greatcoat with shiny gold buttons. The first time I wore it at sea on a coastal voyage to Hamburg in winter, all the other officers and midshipmen laughed and said "Whatever did you buy that for?" They all had army surplus duffel coats which cost a few pounds. I had no answer for them. I suppose the true answer was "I was conned by the outfitters" - but I was not going to admit that.

Many years later, visiting my parents with Ann, my bride to be, I was wearing a rather scruffy gabardine mackintosh. My father was ashamed of me. He said "Come with me," took me into town, with me feeling about 10 years old, he bought me a new overcoat. I was slightly ashamed, but grateful and that overcoat lasted me for many years. It eventually became a bit old and battered.

Years later again, as a lecturer, I had completed my research degree and was very proud to be asked to present a paper at a conference in the splendid building of the Institution of Electrical Engineers, in Savoy Place, just off the Strand in London. There were hundreds of people attending and the lecture went quite well. I had to travel back to Liverpool that evening and needed to leave just before the end. I made my apologies and slipped away. As

I approached the cloakroom, I felt in my pocket. I had lost the cloakroom ticket.

Me (to the cloakroom attendant) "I have lost my cloakroom ticket and need to leave now!"

Cloakroom attendant "I can't let you into the cloakroom, Sir, but if you describe the coat, I will try to find it!" With hundreds of coats for him to choose from, I thought my chances were slim.

Me "It is probably the scruffiest coat in the place"

He came straight back with it. I caught my train. So sometimes it does help if you are dressed to stand out from the crowd!

More Seafaring Stories

1. What is he reading?

Sunday, with Bill Lillie and his family in a Glasgow church. The Minister was reading from the bible. The décor of the church was simple and severe and the members of the congregation were silently following the text in their own bibles. As the Minister came to the bottom of the page, the silence was broken by the sound of dozens of pages being turned. After about another paragraph, there was the noise of a single page being turned, and everyone looked at Bill's father, to try to see what book he was reading!

There was a simple explanation. Bill's father had lived in Argentina in his early years and spoke Spanish. He did not come across many Spanish speakers in his store in Glasgow, so kept up his language skills by following the text in a Spanish bible on Sundays. The page turns were in different places, but I think the rest of the congregation thought he was reading something else.

2. Doctors

French Somaliland had been through a series of local coups and insurrections. One thing that suffers at such times is local health care, and we were warned that going ashore was not good for your health. Even so, we all thought it would be good if the Chief Steward could buy local fresh vegetables and fruit to supplement the frozen food we had in the fridges since we left Liverpool three months before. We took bunkers and filled every corner of the main decks with a "deck cargo" of live cattle (accompanied by their herdsmen) for the voyage up the Red Sea to Suez. Doing your rounds of the deck at 4 am after your watch was more interesting than usual, as you had to negotiate your way through the herd.

We discharged the cattle into lighters in Suez Bay and proceeded into the canal. The Second Steward, who was a likeable fit man in his early thirties, complained of not feeling very well. We had a Male Nurse on board, but as we had been to Djibouti, he decided to ask for a doctor to come on board in Port Said.

The Egyptian doctor examined the Second Steward and said: "It's just 'flu. Give him a 'haspirin' and send him to bed!"

Two days later, as we steamed westward through the Mediterranean, the patient got very much worse and died of yellow fever.

We made arrangements and stopped the ship for a burial at sea, conducted by the ship's Master. The death would be a devastating blow for the Second Steward's family. It also ruined for all the crew the usually happy feelings ("the channels") that normally fill everyone with the thought of being home in a few days. When we arrived in the UK the ship was quarantined - a sad end to the voyage.

3. Dentists

If you are on a long ocean passage and get toothache, there are no dentists to visit, so you put up with painkillers and hope you can see a dentist at the next port. Your kind and compassionate shipmates really enjoy telling you about the dental treatment they have undergone in the past, in out-of-the-way primitive ports and shantytowns. I thought I would be all right because my toothache happened a few days before we arrived in Singapore, a thriving modern city that must have good dentists – I thought. According to some of my colleagues, the company saved a bit of money by using Chinese dentists in a run-down part of the city, who were cruel!

One advantage of having an uncle who was well known in the area was that I got invited to "posh" cocktail parties. I met a lot of interesting people and on this occasion I was talking to an Army Major and mentioned my problem. He said "Don't go to one of the local dentists. My wife is a qualified dentist and I am sure she would be happy to have a look at your tooth and fix things for you!" My visit to her dental surgery the next day was arranged and I thought my luck had really changed when she approached – blonde and beautiful. Then everything changed – I had never suffered so much pain in my life! She may have been beautiful but her cruelty outshone anything the local Chinese Dentists could inflict. I've been suspicious of beautiful blondes ever since.

4. Wreck Removal

Most seafarers complete their careers without being involved in wreck removal. My uncle, Captain Leonard Hatcher, is a Master Mariner, now over 90 years old. He gave me good advice about wreck removal. He joined the harbourmaster's staff in Penang, Malaya at the end of World War 2. A wreck was blocking the channel and the Royal Navy Wreck Removal Squad was busy in Singapore, so he borrowed some explosives, set them in the wreck and set the timer to give himself enough time to return to the surface and get clear. Once in the boat, he could not get the outboard motor to start. His advice to me was "Always have a second means of escape!" In modern parlance – do a proper risk assessment! He just got clear in time. My own life has had some interesting interactions with outboard motors.

Captain Leonard Hatcher - Harbourmaster

5. Seagull Outboard Motors and Reliability

"Seagull" outboard motors were a legend. Ours was no exception. No matter how we mistreated it, dropping it in the sea, storing it in a damp shed without flushing the system out with fresh water, never getting it serviced for

42

years, being a bit cavalier in measuring out the oil/petrol mixture etc. Bring it out in the spring, clean the spark plug, wind the starter cord round the flywheel and off it went! Second pull if not the first one.

It reminded me of the agent I met in Malaya who represented another British engine manufacturer – Listers - in the Far East. In the mid 1950s he had a complaint from a customer in Borneo who owned a sawmill. The other sawmill nearby had a new Japanese engine, and boasted that every time his engine broke down – which was frequently – the local agent had a full set of spares. The Lister man, very hurt, was told by his customer: "The first time my engine broke down, I go to the local agent and he has to send back to the UK for spares. What poor service!" The Lister man, a bit surprised, said, "When did you install your British engine?" The answer "1936!"

At that time there were a number of Japanese and other foreign outboard motors being used around the coast of the UK in summer by fishermen and holidaymakers. They were being caught out when the motor was stopped or broke down at sea and would not restart. Enter upon the scene the Government's Central Office of Information, to make a film on the dangers of unreliable outboard

43

motors. Which outboard did they show breaking down? A British Seagull! When it was pointed out that the British outboards were very reliable, the COI spokesman said "We know that! But the COI is only allowed to feature British equipment in its films!"

Ask anybody in 2008 if they recognise the relative reliability of Japanese and British engines which I describe above and they would shake their heads. But believe me, there was a golden age of British engineering – it finished about 1965.

6. Come for a bike ride?

As a ten / eleven year old in mid-Sussex, I had to cycle three miles from our quiet village, then catch a bus for the remaining seven miles to Collyers Grammar School in Horsham. Moving to Dovercourt in Essex, bikes were still important. Without them, we would have been much more

limited in our ability to roam, meet friends and take part in team games and other activities. Bikes were a part of our lives.

For my brother Robin, bikes became even more of an obsession. We had a young Customs Officer John Pieracini, lodging with us. John was a racing cyclist. Robin was fascinated. Later on, Robin became an accomplished road (and sometimes track) racer.

At seventeen, I went off to sea on my first four-month voyage to Australia. Returning home in the summer of 1953, I was greeted by a smiling Robin who said "Would you like to see my new bike?" He had a shining new drop-handle-barred racing bike, and was obviously very proud of it.

He asked me "Would you like to come for a bike ride with me?"

I said I would. A thoughtful look crossed his face.
He said "We cannot go, Dad has his bike at work".
I said "I don't need Dad's bike, I can use mine."
Looking a bit ashamed, Robin said "You have not got a bike any more, I traded it in to get my new one!"
Seeing our own children grow up, I realise that some respect the property of others, but some are not averse to using other people's property as if it was their own.

7. Figure of Eight

Outward bound to the Far East in the Blue Funnel training ship "Calchas", we had passed Dondra Head, the southern tip of Ceylon, and were heading due east for Malaya. The cadet ship had 22 midshipmen in place of the normal Able Bodied Seamen, Ordinary Seamen and Deck Boys. There was a lot of maintenance work to be done on deck, overhauling cargo gear etc, so the company had installed an "Iron Mike" (automatic steering) on the bridge, to free the wheelman to work on deck. Today, most ships have reliable automatic pilots, but in 1955 they often broke down. When this happened, a midshipman was called to the bridge to steer by hand. On this occasion I was sent to put on clean dungarees and go to the bridge to steer.

The steering was easy. Half a turn to port or starboard to keep the ship on 090 degrees true. Suddenly the wheel spun out of my hand, "hard a starboard" and the ship began a tight turn. The wheel was hard over and would not move. Within a few minutes, I was surrounded by all the "top brass" – Master, First Mate, Second Mate, Chief Engineer, Electrician etc. They stood round and just looked. Eventually, the Chief Engineer said, "There is an imbalance in the oil pressure in the Telemotor (which sends the steering signals down aft to the rudder). Out with his screwdriver,

he attacked a valve and the wheel spun the other way. "Hard a port" and we started to turn tightly the other way.

Meanwhile there were two other ships heading east near us, and they must have been amazed as we did a huge figure eight in our course.

I am ashamed to admit that the ship turning a figure eight with all the top brass standing round, looking wise, but totally impotent, struck me as funny. I laughed. I was sent from the bridge and replaced by a midshipman who did not share my sense of humour.

Homeward Bound

Mostly, on the outward-bound trip, I kept a low profile, rather than getting into scrapes with authority. It was such a low profile, that more than a month into the voyage, when it came to selecting the leading cadet (Bosun's Mate) for the next voyage, the old Bosun did not even know my name. He had to ask someone: "Who's the big fella?" As the selection committee, Master, First Mate and Bosun considered each name amongst the 11 junior midshipmen, his misdemeanours where highlighted and they passed on until they reached me. So I was made Bosun's Mate on the following voyage.

8. Being Responsible for the Sins of Others

All Blue Funnel ships were expected to arrive in our home port of Liverpool gleaming with fresh paint. Unfortunately, midshipmen are not economical when they are painting. They get it on the deck and on themselves. So the cadet ship "Calchas" was getting very short of paint by the time we reached Colombo, homeward bound.

As the pilot boarded, he was escorted to the bridge to meet the Master, Captain Digby Jones.
His first remark was "Good morning, Captain. Who is Digby?"
The Master said : "I am, I suppose, why do you ask?"
Pilot: "Somebody hates you!"
Master "How do you know?"
Pilot: "It is written on the side of your ship!"
At the 2009 reunion of the cadets, Taff Hulland admitted, it was he who painted the message. At the time, as Boatswain's Mate, I was blamed.

We spent the day alongside loading tea and desiccated coconut etc. The pilot came aboard and we pulled off the quay. Many ships' names were painted on the quayside, it is a tradition for the crew, when painting the hull from the quay, to record the ship's name and the date of the visit, usually in letters a foot high or less. On this occasion, the name M.V. "Calchas" was painted in two colours about four feet high with shading that made them stand out as if they were in 3-D. Knowing how short of paint we were, the Master and Mate went ballistic! I got the blame again. I was told to find out who did it, and send them to clean and paint the inside of the focslehead paint store. In the Southwest Monsoon punching into a head sea, this was a very uncomfortable job. The two miscreants were duly despatched to do the nasty deed. An hour or so later, I was sent for by the Master. "Holder" he said "I told you to find out who painted the quayside and make them clear out the foc'sle. I have seen a lot of midshipmen going up forward. Why did you send them all?" He was somewhat nonplussed by my reply "I did not send them, Sir! They volunteered, because they said it was unfair to penalise the ones who were painting on the quay. They all agreed that, if they had been doing that job, they would have painted the ship's name too!"

9. The Ship's Magnetic Compass

In the 1920s and 30s most people studying for a Master Mariner's Certificate of Competency dreaded the Magnetic Compass. It had been much easier on wooden ships. Steel ships were themselves big magnets and affected their own compasses. Not only were they permanent magnets, but they also had magnetic effects induced by the earth's magnetic field, which changed wherever you went across the world. The scientists had analysed all these effects and provided a binnacle with fore-and-aft and athwartships permanent magnet correctors, and so-call soft-iron "Flinders Bar" and "Kelvin's Balls," to correct for induced magnetism.

Even in the 1960s it was regarded as a difficult subject, brilliantly taught at Sir John Cass College in London by Captain Klinkert, who with his colleague Captain Grant wrote the definitive book on the subject. Many mariners who had passed the examination described the first few weeks of the course like a thick fog, which suddenly cleared when all the various coefficients and corrections "fell into place". I was lucky, the fog cleared early because I enjoyed scientific subjects. For some the fog never cleared at all.

In 1963, fresh from the classroom, I was sailing between Harwich and Rotterdam on the British Rail cargo ships, which had no gyro and relied, like most coasters at that time, on the magnetic compass. I was early on one return trip and decided to carry out a full "compass adjustment" swing, steaming on all compass headings, taking bearings of a fixed object and carrying out the analysis of the results. It worked out well and showed that, on east – west courses the error was very small, but if the ship went north or south there would be a "huge" 5 degree error. I proudly showed my results to the Master when he came on the bridge. He said "We don't bother with that, son! The shore-based Compass Adjuster comes aboard once a year and does his stuff – we don't touch it!" As the ship was about to steam north to drydock in Immingham, I hope my observations helped it keep on course instead of veering off into the North Sea.

How Did We Do?
As Head of Department, I had a long letter from a former student serving on a bulk carrier. They had been to Port Hedland in Western Australia to load iron pyrites. Nobody on board was aware of the magnetic characteristics of the cargo and they did not put canvas covers over the gyrocompass, radars, and other equipment. When they sailed, the magnetic dust had permeated every nook and cranny and nothing worked. Thank goodness for the magnetic compass, well-

boxed chronometers and their sextants. Knowing which course to steer was still not easy – the ship was full of a magnetic cargo!

The Second Mate, remembering his recent Magnetic Compass lectures at the Polytechnic, supervised a full compass adjustment "swing" and produced a Deviation Card with which to apply corrections. They made it round the Cape of Good Hope and back to Europe with this very basic equipment. He then sent the letter to us saying "How did we do?" In terms of homework marks, I think they had earned 100%. The Government Department of Transport Examiners agreed.

10. Guilty Conscience

We had a Liverpool crew on the M.V. "Rhexenor." I was talking to the ship's carpenter who was busy in his workshop, when I noticed that he had a brand new Bridges Power Tool kit. I asked "Is that part of the ship's equipment?" "No" he said: "My family gave it to me as a present." I admired it.

Some time later the carpenter came to my cabin to ask me something and noticed that I had a very nice large Three Wave Band Radio. It had allowed me to listen to short-wave overseas broadcasts.

The conversation went like this:
Chippy; "That is a nice radio! I have always wanted a decent radio. Would you like to swap it for my Power Tool kit?"

Me: "It was a nice radio, but one of the valves has gone and it doesn't work any more!"

Chippy; "That doesn't worry me – would you like to swap!"

Me; "Yes, but I think you would be getting a very poor bargain!"

Chippy: "I don't! When we have a day off on Sundays, I sit on my settee and think of all the things my family expect me to make with my new tool kit. If I had your radio, I would look at it, think 'it doesn't work' and fall asleep with a clear conscience."

The swap was duly made and for many years I used the kit – not only a power drill, but a bench stand, lathe, saw and various other bits of equipment.

I wonder what he told his family or if he ever got the radio fixed.

11. Lost for Words

Homeward Bound from the Far East, rather than calling in to Aden for bunkers we went to Djibouti in former French Somaliland instead. The attraction from the Company's point of view was a deck cargo of live cattle to be delivered in the port of Suez, before going through the Suez Canal. When we arrived, we berthed alongside a large open quay and in a short time we saw a large herd of cattle approaching, headed by a very  tall and imposing Somali tribesman in native dress. All the ship's crew lined the ship's rail to watch as I, as the duty officer, marched up the quay to greet them. Suddenly, the tribesman stopped, so did the cattle behind him. I stopped too.

He raised his right arm above his head and said in a loud voice:

"God Bless Queen Elizabeth!"

My immediate thought was that I should bless his Head of State, but with all the military coups and local wars, I was unsure whom to bless. My mind was racing, because getting it wrong might cause a diplomatic incident. Eventually, I chickened out, put my right hand up and shouted:

"Thank You!"

They resumed their approach.

Phew!

12. Mistaken Identity

The cadet training ship "Diomed" had 22 midshipmen on board in place of the normal complement of ABs (Able Bodied Seamen), OSs (Ordinary Seamen) and Deck Boys. I was Third Mate. It was November 1959. We were in Kobe, Japan loading cargo for the UK. I was on the boat deck when one of the other officers came up to me and said "You had better get down to the gangway sharpish. There is a young Japanese woman asking for you, and she won't take no for an answer!"

As I made my way down to the gangway, my mind was racing to try to think who it might be. We had been in port about 24 hours and the day before a group of us had hired a taxi and taken a trip up into the mountains above the city. My only other trips ashore were to do a bit of shopping and to post letters home to Ann and the family. I wondered who this person could be, who was demanding to see "The Third Mate." She was an attractive young lady, but I had never seen her before in my life. She said "No! No! You are not the Third Mate!" I insisted that I was. A swift piece of detective work soon solved the case. One of the midshipmen had danced with her in a bar the evening before, and in order to impress her, had promoted himself to Third Mate! Of course, although I had been visiting Japan for six years and had met several young ladies, I was not really worried.

Another Young Lady

Many years later when I was a senior member of the teaching staff at Liverpool Polytechnic, I passed someone in the 6th Floor corridor who said "By the way, there is an attractive young Filipino lady waiting for you in your office. She knew all about you and asked for you by name!" My mind went back to the days before I was married and had enjoyed dancing and socialising in the Philippines. I had particularly enjoyed Cebu, where the atmosphere was

Laundry Woman in Cebu

55

very friendly and relaxed. Could it be another case of mistaken identity? I recalled that the "Phemius" had tied up very near the town and a group of girls came down to see the ship as it pulled away from the quay. I remembered one in particular who stood up to her full height and shouted "Shoeshine! I want my panties!" Captain McMillan was not amused and junior engineer Mr Shoesmith made a swift exit down the Engineroom. But, back to the present dilemma. I did not recognised the well-spoken and confident young lady in my office. I was very interested to hear that she had obtained my name through nautical papers and publications. The Philippine Government was trying to raise standards in its nautical colleges and decreed that no one could be principal of a school unless they had a degree in education. Her father was the principal of their small school and he had just the normal Master Mariner qualifications and not a degree, so he sent his daughter to the USA to become a "Master of Education" and they ran the school together. She just wanted my advice.

13. Over-Carried Cargo

One of the problems with general cargo ships that carry a huge number of different items of cargo, is that you sometimes miss one or two items that should be discharged, and over-carry them to the next port. A real nuisance having to discharge them at the next port and get the agent to send them back to their proper destination. So we always had a very careful search before sailing. We had done just that in Hong Kong before sailing for Shanghai.

When Communist China re-opened to shipping from the West, the authorities were very suspicious. After we had sailed, we had yet another message from Blue Funnel Line Headquarters in Liverpool, telling us that absolutely every item of cargo on board had to be put on manifests and declared; otherwise we would be in trouble.

At sea, the Chief Officer sent the deck officers and midshipmen down into the holds to double check. We reported back to him that we had found one case of Hong Kong cargo in No 2 Lower Hold.

"Don't worry" said the Chief Officer "We had the same problem last voyage, so we brought the item up to the officer's accommodation, labelled it as ship's stores and we got away with it!"

Pointing, he said "Just bring it up and put it in that locker." We replied, "We cannot do that, sir. It weighs 25 tons!"

We went back down into the hold and removed the destination label on the case, hoping the authorities would think it was for Japan. They did not notice it, so we were not arrested and were able to deliver it two weeks late when we called at Hong Kong homeward bound.

14. "Yam Sing!" or "Mind the Wire"

From the Guide Book: "At the end of the meal be prepared to "yam sing" or down your drink in one gulp. When one person stands and announces "yam sing" as he drains his brandy glass, he is issuing a challenge for you to do likewise and failure to follow would cause great offence".

The old Blue Funnel ship "Phemius" was a challenge to us all. Built in 1926, she had had a hard life as she neared her 50th birthday. We had a Chinese crew and everyone got on well together. We were in Bangkok for Chinese New Year and everything ground to a halt for the three days of celebration. All the officers were invited down aft to the crew accommodation to celebrate the New Year. The first day it was the deck crew, the second day the engine room ratings and the third day the Catering Department. The process was the same. Late afternoon, the officers crowded into the crew messroom. The first crew member appeared, filled the officer's whiskey glasses and his own, held his glass up high, shouted "Yam Sing!" and downed the contents in one, at which we all had to do the same. The second crew member then appeared with a bottle of whiskey, the process was repeated, then the third etc. After about four glasses of "fire water" my throat was on fire. I accepted the offer of a cool beer to put the fire out. After the last crew member left, we made our way unsteadily back to our accommodation up forward. On one day I was the last to leave and the other officers were all gathered outside the forward accommodation. I had forgotten the complicated wires rigged for discharging a heavy lift when cargo work resumed.

As I started to move along the centrecastle deck towards them, they shouted something. They repeated it and I could just about make out that they were saying "Mind the wire!" My mind was somewhat befuddled. This next thing I knew, my ankle hit a greasy guy wire, which ran across from the derrick. I fell flat on my face. It took a long time to live that one down.

15. S.S. "Rhesus"

Having been Third Mate for a long time, I was delighted to get my first appointment as Second Mate. My first ship was to be the steamship "Rhesus". She was a Victory Ship built in the USA during World War II. Much faster than the Liberty ships, they had steam turbine main engines and were capable of doing 17 knots. When I joined, unfortunately, there was a bit of a recession and s.s. "Rhesus" was not going anywhere – she was laid up in the River Fal in Cornwall, by King Harry Ferry. Nevertheless, the two stripes were sewn on and I went off to join her, taking Ann with me.

I left Ann in a hotel in Truro and got a taxi to King Harry Ferry and a small boat came over to take me on board. I was welcomed by the small and very relaxed "lay-up" crew who immediately said there was no need for me to stay on board overnight – so I made my way back to Truro. It was dark. I crept up to our room. It was locked, so I knocked gently. No response. I knocked more loudly – still no response from Ann, but the chap in the room opposite asked if there was a problem. I said "No problem!" and knocked more loudly. Several other doors opened and a crowd gathered. They said "Is your wife a heavy sleeper?" I replied "I don't know!" That raised a few eyebrows. The

chap in the next room said "Would you like to knock on the adjoining wall – the noise doesn't matter – everyone is awake now." Still no response. The manager then brought a passkey and as soon as the door opened and light fell on her face, Ann woke up and said sleepily "Oh, it's you!" We said good night and went to bed. Next morning we crept down to breakfast sheepishly and told them we had not been married very long!

I had learned that light would wake my new wife but she could sleep through very loud noises!

After that day we moved to the old pub at Malpas with the other members of the crew whose wives were with them. The "workers" went off down the river to the ship after breakfast in a large dinghy with an outboard motor. The pub did not have any more double beds and it was cold, so we snuggled up on one of the twin beds. Each night I found my pyjamas had been placed under the pillow of the other bed.

Eventually the "maid" gave up and put both sets of nightwear under the same pillow. There was a wonderful party at New Year and a lady from the village came up to us, winked and said "You don't know me, but I know about you!" She explained that she made our beds.

Once a week a boat came up from Falmouth to take us down to do get stores and carry out necessary official reporting. The boatman said "Proper Job" after every sentence or question and so that became his name. I was told to go to the Mercantile Marine Office to collect Admiralty Notices to  Mariners so that we could keep our charts and publications up-to-date ready to sail when the company found a cargo for us. The Shipping Master gave me the documents and asked me to sign. With a flourish I signed Leonard Holder, Second Officer, s.s. "Rhesus". The Shipping Master was distraught. "Oh dear, Oh dear!" he said "I wish you hadn't done that!" When I enquired what, he said "Put Second Officer!" He explained that his instructions said that the notices had to be signed for by a RESPONSIBLE OFFICER (Master or Chief Officer). I felt deflated. I still had not made it to that status.

16. Illustrations

Perhaps I am lazy or unimaginative, but I like books that have pictures in them, rather than reams of text. I am not alone. Since I became Chairman of Videotel Marine International I have written a regular personal newsletter about shipboard training to the masters and crewmembers of thousands of ships. It started as a normal letter – just words. When I was visiting Japan, I asked several people whether they liked the letter. The Japanese people all looked at the floor, rather embarrassed and said softly: "Too many words, not enough pictures!" So now the newsletter has fewer words and many more pictures – a useful piece of advice.

When I wrote a guide to good shipboard training entitled "Training Onboard", I thought it needed to be livened up with illustrations. I thought back to my time at sea, when a fellow officer drew cartoons on any available piece of paper. The fourth mate of MV Machaon, Alan Hare, did not get on very well with Mr D.K. Dunlop, the Mate. They shared a watch. As part of his duties, Alan had to record hatch temperatures to make sure the cargo was being properly ventilated. The surrounding air temperature was put in the record under the heading of AMBIENT temperature. We discovered that Mr Dunlop had never come across the word "ambient." So Alan invented a little cartoon character called "An Angry Ambient." This character would turn up on temperature charts, rough log books, cargo notebooks etc usually with a thought bubble which referred obliquely to one of Mr Dunlop's less favourable characteristics (he had many). It drove Mr D. up the wall.

I contacted Alan and asked him if he would like to illustrate my new book on training. It was just the right moment. He had been made redundant from his command of a refrigerated cargo ship, for daring to suggest that being in command of a ship on which the Chinese crew spoke no English and he spoke no Chinese was dangerous. Actually the second steward did understand a few words of English, and at the start of the voyage Alan wrote down a list of all the orders he might want to give during the voyage, and the second steward wrote his best effort in Chinese alongside it. Each morning was like ordering at a Chinese restaurant. "Today we will have order numbers 34, 76 and 104". Then you waited to see what happened. Alan thought that was dangerous, the company disagreed. Anyway, their loss was my gain and Alan's relevant and amusing cartoons made the book much more readable than it would otherwise have been.

Alan's new job was driving high speed ferries in the Solent. He told me that during the Cowes Week regatta, his way ahead was often barred by an impenetrable mass of yachts. One advantage of the high speed ferries was that they could stop very quickly. I asked if crash stops caused any problems. "Not for me!" he said, "But before we get going again, I have to wait a few minutes for the old ladies to find their false teeth!"

Alan has contributed more Angry Ambients for this book:

A SELECTION of "ANGRY AMBIENTS"

17. Best Value

Joining British Railways ferry Services at Harwich in 1962, as Second Mate with a Master's Certificate I earned £14.10s a week. People stayed on those ships with such poor wages because they wanted to be near home with their families. There were other compensations too. As a railway employee, you received reduced fare "privileged" rail tickets and a number of free passes each year for you and your family, and one free pass per year on continental railways.

1962 – 1963 was a harsh winter and people talked a lot about the summer and holidays. A lot of the people apparently took their holidays in a very small town right down in the south of Greece. As so many people chose it, I thought it must be a very attractive place, so I asked: "What are the attractions?" The reply gave me food for thought: "It is a small place, not very nice, no good beaches, poor hotels, very little to do, but it is the furthest place you can reach on your free continental rail pass!" With all Europe to choose from, it surprised me that getting best value for a "freebie" was so important!

18. A Surprisingly Fast Passage

The winter of 1962 /63 was very cold. The rivers of Europe were full of ice – even the Scheldt and the Stour at Harwich. The 14 knot British Rail ferry "Colchester" made its way down the Scheldt from Antwerp, pushing though the ice flows past Terneuzen and Flushing, out towards the North Sea where it went "full away" - full speed for Harwich.

In the engineroom, the Duty Engineer noticed that the propeller revolutions had fallen below normal, so he cranked up the fuel supply a notch or two. The ship started to vibrate a bit more than usual. On the bridge, the Second Mate was surprised at how fast the ship was going – he noticed the vibrations too. The ship was doing over 16 knots. We only just made it to Harwich – we nearly ran out of fuel.

On investigation it was discovered that the propeller had hit the ice and bent in such a way that it had changed the "pitch" giving higher speed for lower revolutions, but hopelessly out of balance. So the ship was put out of service and sent to drydock to get the propeller fixed – expensive!

19. Minimum Manning

In the 21st Century people are at last asking why ship's crews get fatigued and make mistakes. It is very often caused by crew numbers being reduced further and further until there are just not enough people to do everything that has to be done.

Back in the 1960's some ships were over-manned. I give as an example the two small British Rail cargo ships "Isle of Ely" and "Colchester" which ran between Harwich and Rotterdam and Harwich and Antwerp. Having departed from Antwerp, I was on watch going down the River Scheldt. The pilot saw the Bosun and crew tidying up and washing the decks, the helmsman, the lookout, the steward who brought him coffee etc. He said "So many people! I don't think I have seen the same person twice. How many crew members do you have?" Now, my first though is 21, but perhaps it was only 12 or 15. At that stage I knew the number and told the pilot.

"Wow!" He said "No wonder you British cannot compete in coastal shipping! If this was a Dutch coaster, there would be five people at most."

We were passing Flushing at that time. The pilot added "Mind you, small crews can have their drawbacks. The other day, near here, on a Dutch coaster, we suddenly ran into thick fog. I rushed to the telegraph to ring down to the Engine Room for 'Dead Slow Ahead.' The man on the wheel said, "There is no point ringing that! I am the Engineer!"

20. The Big Freeze February 1963 Harwich to Rotterdam

A news item on 22nd February 1963 said "The Great Freeze immobilised most shipping activities on the Medway and the Thames. At Sun Pier, Chatham, the pack ice covered the full width of the river. The sea at Whitstable and Pegwell Bay was also frozen." In fact, all the North Sea ports were affected by fresh and sea water ice. There was floating sea ice in Harwich Harbour.

I was serving on the British Rail cargo ship "Colchester" on the runs between Harwich and Antwerp and Harwich and Rotterdam. Reporting to the Despatching Department at Parkeston Quay, I was told that we would be sailing at 9 p.m. for Rotterdam. The Master, only recently promoted, was worried that we would be heading straight into Force 8 (Gale Force) winds off the frozen continent, and the forecast was for the wind to increase to Force 9

or 10 (Storm Force). He probably should have refused to sail, but a few weeks earlier with an almost identical forecast, another Master had refused to sail, and the wind had decreased to Force 7 or 6 during the night, and he had been hauled over the coals by the Marine Superintendent. Given a choice between the weather and Captain Wright, our Master decided to sail.

We normally worked "Half Ways", splitting the overnight passage in two, the Mate keeping watch for half and the Second Mate the rest, or vice versa. Half way was marked on the chart. The small container ship was pitching and shuddering so much as we headed into the gale, that we were nowhere near half way when I was called to relieve the Mate. Up in the wheelhouse, the windows were covered in frozen sea spray as the bow buried itself into each wave and flung spray over the masthead. Dawn broke and a very brave Able Seaman went up on the Monkey Island (above the bridge) and leaned over to scrape the windows clear. By 0830 hours, I was ready for my breakfast. I sent the standby man down to the galley, which he found was empty, with no breakfast being prepared.

He returned to the bridge and reported: "The cook is in his bunk. He says that he only cooks in port. He says that he was terribly seasick deep sea and joined the railway ships because they spent days in port and nights at sea. If you get the ship into port, he will cook your breakfast!" We did not get in until 11am. In the interim the AB fired up the galley and provided hot tea and soup for us all. It was one of the best breakfasts I have tasted.

When we got into Rotterdam, it took us more than a day to chip the ice off the decks and hatchcovers and discharge the cargo. I arrived home eventually to a surprised Ann who greeted me with "Where have you been? I expected you two days ago. I thought the railway ships provided a regular service!"

21. The Trades Unions at Harwich

In the 1950s and 60s the Trades Unions were very powerful in Harwich. In order to tie up the ships at Parkeston Quay, five people were required in the shore gang. It only took two people to do the work, but all five had to be there. If one had gone off for a cup or tea or a comfort break, the ships could not be tied up. When number five resumed his place, sitting idly on a bollard or other handy seat, the team swung into action.

Arriving Early

In addition, the ships were told not to arrive before the starting time for the gang – 6 a.m. and not a minute before. As the ship approached the berth and the bow got close enough to the quay, the bosun would throw the heaving line onto the shore at the feet of the mooring gang. The foreman of the gang would look at his watch, and if it was 5.59 a.m. the gang would watch the heaving line as it fell back into the river. Frustrating, but our fault for arriving early.

Sailing Late

If you were called down to the quay to join the ship and the ship did not sail on time, the Union had negotiated a "Late Sailing" bonus. Although I never did it myself, I understand on good authority, that crewmembers would go into the Captain's cabin and push his clock forward a few minutes to make sure we sailed late. Not hard to do, as he was on the bridge. What was much trickier was going into his cabin when he was asleep to push the minute hand back again.

Disturbance of Rest

Those people serving on the train ferries from Harwich to Zeebrugge were looked after by the Trade Union too. Because it takes a very short time to unload the four lines of railway wagons and load another four, they had short turn-round times. If the ship turned round and sailed again within four hours, the crew received a "Disturbance of Rest" bonus. It became an expected part of their income. When container trade to Antwerp picked up the spare train ferry was sent on that run. Not designed for containers, it took ages to load and discharge them onto and from the train deck – no quick turn rounds there. The crew had much more rest, but payday was a bit thin without the bonus. So the Union negotiated a "Bonus In Lieu of Disturbance of Rest Bonus". Incredible?

Weekends Off

I was amazed at the generosity of my shipmates when it came to weekend working. I worked Monday to Friday and they said "You are not long married and you have a young wife and family, we will volunteer to do the weekend shifts and let you spend the weekend with your family" I thought "What nice people!" It was not until much later that I discovered, because of the Union agreement they earned more over the weekend than I did by working all the rest of the week. Still, it was nice to have weekends at home.

More from Liverpool and the Polytechnic

1. Car Sharing

Commuting from the Wirral through the old Mersey Tunnel to Liverpool Polytechnic was a nightmare for us. It caused real nightmares for the Head of Department, who imagined rooms full of students waiting to be taught and most of his staff stuck in the tunnel. Today, with two tunnels, there is less of a crush.

Doing our bit to help solve the problem, three of us did a car-share, Keith Jones, Alan Bole and myself. As I lived furthest away, it was usually my car that we used. We became a bit worried when news items on the radio said that anyone who was paid for petrol by a car-sharer would be regarded as plying for hire and in breach of the insurance rules. Since owning my first car in 1957, I had always been insured by Royal Insurance. However, as we were friends we did not think it mattered if Keith or Alan paid for the odd gallon and tunnel toll.

It was a four-seater car, and Alan asked if we would give his neighbour a lift into Liverpool some mornings. I agreed and when it became fairly regular we suggested he might like to contribute to the costs, which he did. It was not until later that I realised he worked at "the sand-castle" – Royal Insurance's Headquarters in Liverpool. As far as I know he did not "rat" on us.

Speed Traps

Until 1975 we lived on Pensby Road, which was a busy thoroughfare. We were on a long straight hill and the police often set up a speed trap outside our house during the day. Ann watched them and noticed that young men were always given speeding tickets, but attractive young ladies in short skirts were not.

At this time we were giving another of Alan's neighbours a lift to Bootle. I innocently retold Ann's tale of the speed trap and a very loud and angry female voice from the back seat said "Well! That sort of thing might happen on the Wirral, but it certainly doesn't happen in Bootle!"

When I asked where she wanted to be dropped off in Bootle, she said "At the police station!" I had not realised she was a policewoman!

2. The Raid

We were returning to the main Polytechnic in Byrom Street from the little Radar School on the edge of Gladstone Dock. There were four of us, Keith Jones, Alan Bole, Rex Pelling and myself, all radar lecturers., all quite big men. Well, Rex Pelling was not that big but it was getting dark. On the way to the Radar School in the morning one of us, who was looking for a second-hand car, had seen a likely vehicle on a forecourt in Scotland Road and we were all going to have a look at it.

When we arrived, the car salesman had been standing in the showroom. When we walked in, he was nowhere to be seen. Eventually we found him cowering behind his desk: he was trembling, white as a sheet and obviously terrified. We asked, "What is the matter?"

He said "All I saw was a large car screeching to a halt, four doors being flung open and four big men leaping out and coming towards me! I though it was a raid!"

When he recovered his composure we looked at the car, but it was not what we wanted.

We made a mental note to stop gently and get out one at a time in future!

3. Traffic Hazards on Scotland Road

Whilst teaching at the Radar School in Bootle, Alan Bole and I used to drive into Liverpool down Scotland Road towards the Mersey Tunnel. In the late afternoon it was always busy, and in the 1960s there were lots of children living in the area, and no over bridges or tunnels for pedestrians. Amidst all the heavy traffic young children were often to be seen dashing across through the crush of buses, lorries and cars. On one occasion, we were horrified to see a scruffy little lad of about five years old, dragging what must have been his sister of about three, through the traffic. We watched anxiously until they reached the other side. We let out a huge sigh of relief. A few moments later, we were horrified to see the same two crossing back through the traffic. We then both realised, and Alan said "They are not crossing the road. They are playing a game. It is called 'chicken.'" In 2010, when parents are criticised for wrapping their children in cotton wool, the parents of those two might teach us a thing or two?

4. Girls at Sea

When I went to sea, it was a man's world. Later on, young ladies started to take up careers at sea. They were some of our best students – better than the boys – they had to be to survive.

On one occasion I had an SOS from a friend who was a shipmaster on a large container ship in Japan. His daughter, who was 17, had suddenly decided to give up her academic career and go to sea as a cadet. He asked if I could have a word with her and change her mind.

As we chatted, each ploy I tried was countered. I said it was a hard life, unsuitable for girls. She said "I have been to sea with my father, so I know what it is like". I said "Being on board as the Captain's daughter, you will not have had to crawl round amongst cockroaches cleaning the bilges". She said she did not mind cockroaches. Eventually, knowing she was in the final year of A Levels, I said "What subjects are you taking?" When she told me they were "arts" subjects, History and English, I played my trump card. "Well, I am sorry, you would need Mathematics, so you cannot go to sea!" Even though she was half way through her second year in the sixth form, she took mathematics and passed that as well as her original A levels. She went to sea, studied on the degree course with us at the Polytechnic (getting a First Class Honours) in addition to her professional qualifications as a Navigating Officer. She married a marine engineer who also had a First Class Honours degree. Lynne Cook (nee Belk) was a very capable young lady!

Career Choices

As Admissions Tutor for the BSc in Maritime Studies, I vetted application forms and interviewed potential students. A young lady arrived on our doorstep with very fixed ideas on what she wanted to be. She had done her homework. She said "I do not want to go to sea, but I want to study navigation and meteorology and work in an office ashore routing ships across the oceans."
I said "There are only two organisations in the UK which do that, the Meteorological Office in Bracknell and Ocean Routes in Aberdeen. They each have a small staff and only recruit a new person every two or three years. You are very unlikely to get one of those jobs. "I advise you to take a look at a wider range of careers or I will not offer you a place on the course!" She said that she came from the Lake District and there was no way she was going to end up like her friends, as a chambermaid clearing up after visitors in a boarding house. She said "I know my rights! If I have the right A levels I will insist that you take me." "Well!" I said "Don't complain to me if you are disappointed at the end of the course."

She joined the course and was successful in the first two years. In the middle of her final year, I was in London at a conference when a friend from Ocean Routes approached me. He said "We need to recruit someone to do weather routing. They do not have to be seafarers, but should have studied navigation and meteorology. Have you got anyone finishing in the summer?" I told him to hold the post for me, not advertise it, I had just the right person.

I hurried back to Liverpool and told the young lady that her dream had come true, I had found just the right job for her. She looked me straight in the eye and said "I've changed my mind!" Egg all over my face and I had to make excuses to Ocean Routes. The young lady went on to become a ship manager and charterer. She made her mark at the Polytechnic by getting staff and students from the Polytechnic involved with Liverpool University Gilbert and Sullivan Society – a great person to have around.

5. Identical Twins

In recent years multiple births as a result of fertility treatment are not unusual. We never had triplets or quadruplets to deal with at the Polytechnic; we just had identical twins in the BSc Class. I had heard stories about telepathy between twins and the fact that some twins feel and think the same as their opposite number.

I set homework for the navigation class and the twins handed in answers that were very similar – almost identical in fact. I asked them to come and see me, and asked if they had copied from one another. They said they had not! They did admit to chatting about the work before they sat down to write their individual answers, and I explained that, on that evidence, I would reduce the marks I gave them because they had colluded.

In the end of year examinations, which were closely invigilated, the twins were seated on opposite sides of the room and there was no way they could copy from one another. They chose to answer the same questions and their answers were almost identical. They were given full credit for what they had written, of course. This phenomenon set me thinking that I had penalised them unfairly in their homework marks earlier in the year. Very worried, I went back and restored the marks that I had earlier reduced, to see if the penalty would deprive them of a certain Class of Honours Degree. Fortunately the change did not make a difference to their degrees. They went away happy. I was relieved!

6. Cheating – Or Not?

I had a phone call from the Department of Transport Examiner in Liverpool to say one of our students had been expelled from the examination for cheating. I was surprised, because the student, from Egypt, had no need to cheat. He had worked hard and would have passed unless he was very unfortunate with the questions that came up. He insisted that he had not been cheating and appealed.

At the appeal the evidence against him was cited: the repetition in his answers, of pages of text and diagrams from the textbooks, word for word without any errors. They showed the textbooks and his answers. The Liverpool Examiner said no one could possibly remember so much text and he must have had "crib" sheets from which to copy, though they did not find any in the examination room.

The Chief Examiner, who conducted the appeal said "Did you cheat?"
The student said "No, I didn't!"

The Liverpool Examiner said "You must have cheated!"
Impasse.

The student himself suggested a solution. He said "Take away all the papers and books and give me a pen and a blank sheet of paper." They did. He proceeded to reproduce the textbook details retained in his "photographic memory". The examiners reversed their decision and passed him immediately. They were very embarrassed and asked me not to tell anyone.

I almost kept my promise – until now!

7. Marking Correspondence Courses

When a student passed his or her Second Mates Examination, Liverpool Polytechnic offered a correspondence course for First Mates and likewise for Master when they cleared that hurdle. Most seafarers are not bookworms; they are very practical hands-on people. The idea of sitting in your cabin poring over books does not excite them. Excitement is in their surroundings and the people they meet. The courses were very cheap. Many people, inspired after their recent academic success, bought them. Virtually nobody got beyond Lesson 1. We did not hassle them. At the price they were paying, we could not really afford the staff time to mark hundreds of answers.

Starting a Graduate Entry scheme for the Merchant Navy with Blue Star Line in the 1970s changed all that. They learned quickly and were keen to communicate. One young man wrote to me from the Pacific Coast of the USA and said: "I have only two problems in learning to do this job. In forty years at sea, the Master and Chief Engineer have absorbed a wealth of knowledge, which they do not realise they have. First problem: Getting them to realise how much they know! Second problem: Getting them to pass it on to me! Once I can solve the first problem, the second should be easy."

They used a navigation text book written by George Earl and Frank Main of South Shields College. Frank was now my Head of Department. When the graduates sent back their correspondence course answers they were in two parts 1. Answers to the questions 2. Corrections to the textbook. Frank took it all in good part and thanked them.

At that time I was doing consultancy work on port approaches and traffic management systems. I invited the graduates to choose a port they visited and describe the navigational aids and port traffic system. The answers were many and varied and of very high standard. I remember one trainee described what went on as his ship entered Capetown. He then went ashore and interviewed people in the Port Control Centre and described the same passage from their point of view. Brilliant!

One answer came from the Caribbean, where the ship was running between a Latin American port and the East Coast of the USA with bananas. He described the Caribbean port approach, and in particular the lighthouse at the entrance to the port, which was an excellent navigation mark "except on Thursdays." I thought he was joking, so asked some of the other Blue Star officers about this strange remark. They told me "That is no joke. Everyone on that run knows the lighthouse keeper gets paid on Thursdays. He always gets drunk and nine times out of ten forgets to switch the light on!" Case closed.

8. Asking for References: Head of Department

Shortly after taking over as Head of Maritime Studies, Peter Smeaton, and another staff member, came into my office with a camera and tripod.

I said "Why are you taking my photograph?"

Peter replied: "For your retirement."

Me: "Why now? I have only just got the job, I am not thinking of retiring!"

Peter: "When your predecessor, Frank Main, took over as Head he was young-looking and carefree. When we took his picture a few weeks ago, he looked old and tired. He didn't look like the man we remembered over the years.

We think the job will wear you down too, so we thought we would take your photograph before you are old and haggard!"

Being Head of Department has its pitfalls, not least managing work and leisure time. For many years, I was a member of Wirral Choral Society and also Heswall and District Arts Association. Both used to arrange musical performances in Birkenhead and the Wirral, and many of the audiences were friends and families of those involved. I had to sell my share of the tickets.

A conversation I overheard between two members of my staff in the Department at the Polytechnic caused me amazement and some concern. Coming up "on the blind side" of two members of staff standing outside my office, I heard:

First staff member (pointing towards my office) "Don't ask him for a reference!".

Second member "Why not?"

First member "You have to buy tickets for his b....... choral society!"

Oops!

9. Who is in Charge?

Some people still think it is the Chief Executive or Managing Director who runs a successful company. In fact, for a long time, I thought that too. I was in my mid-40s when someone whispered in my ear "If you want a company to do something, it is no use asking the Managing Director, ask his secretary!"

Carrying out research for the Government, it was necessary to consult the senior managers of a number of shipping companies. Some were very helpful, some were too busy to be bothered. The managing director of a company based on the River Medway was helpful, but he was too busy to respond to my questions. Each time I rang him, he would promise to do it next day, but it never happened. Recalling the advice about secretaries, the next time, instead of asking for him, I asked to talk to his secretary. She said "I am a bit embarrassed that he has kept you waiting. I will see he responds to you. In fact, I make you a promise – I won't let him go home tonight until he has done it." I thanked her, and she kept her promise. There is real power for you.

As Head of Maritime Studies at Liverpool Polytechnic, I thought I was in charge. It was not until I was very close to retirement that I realised that the only person who really knew what I was doing, where everything was and what I should do next, was Barbara Lyons my secretary, to whom I am most grateful.

References

I remember feeling very hurt when Barbara said "You write lousy references!" Most of the members of staff who moved into higher level posts in other colleges seemed to be happy about my references, so I said "What is wrong with them? I always tell people about the strengths of the person and never place too much emphasis on the weaknesses."

That's just it, she said "It is what you don't say that people are interested in when they read a reference. If you don't say they are always punctual, people think they are always late. If you don't say they are sober, people assume they are drunk. If you don't say they are industrious, people will assume they are lazy."

From then on, when evaluating references for people applying to join us, I started to read between the lines. Thank you again, Barbara.

10. A Journey into Welsh

Communication with potential seafaring recruits and degree students from North Wales was hampered because I did not speak Welsh. I went to Wales in support of a Merchant Navy recruitment group, and as each potential applicant sat in front of me, I told them about the courses. A large lad sat down in front of me.

I spoke for two or three minutes and he issued one word: "Cook!"

I spoke for another two or three minutes and asked if he had any questions. He replied "Cook!" From this I gathered that he wanted to be a ship's cook, so I pointed him in the direction of the British Shipping Federation.

Thinking about it, I was determined to do better next time. I produced a tape-slide programme to tell visitors about the college, the courses and opportunities for working together. I asked our Welsh-speaking lecturer, Percy Owen, to put the commentary in Welsh. He agreed, but we ran in to a problem with the custodians of the language. There is no Welsh expression for "satellite navigation". You must not use an English word or make up your own Welsh word. Druids are the custodians of knowledge, language and mythic lore at the heart of the culture of Welsh people. A small group of Druids make up new Welsh words. As society and technology changes a lot of new words are required. There was such a long queue that we had to abandon the idea.

11. The British Council: Home and Away

The British Council aims to strengthen understanding and trust between and within different cultures. They support people striving for better-informed, more inclusive societies that accept, respect and welcome each other. I have met British Council representatives abroad and found them to be intelligent, energetic, committed and keen to help the people in the countries to which they are assigned.

I have also met representatives from the British Council headquarters in the UK. They are not the same. I will give an example. As a course tutor in Liverpool, I met visitors from overseas. Some spoke good English, others struggled. I noticed that many visitors from the Arabic countries, particularly important senior people, listened intently to presentations in English, obviously struggled with some of the words, and did not ask any questions. I asked our Arabic-speaking lecturer, Dr Samir Mankabady to voice the tape-slide programme about the college and courses, in Arabic. It was an immediate success. The next Arab visitors were relaxed as they watched, and asked (in English) a lot of questions afterwards. Success!

I showed the programme to visitors from the British Council. They were very interested. They said "We have never though of doing that. May we borrow the slides and audio tapes?" I readily agreed.

About three months later, I had not heard from them, and we had another important Arab group arriving. I rang the lady at Spring Gardens in London. She said "Ah Yes! I remember. We thought it was such a good idea, but when we got back to headquarters, we did not know what to do with it!" I asked if I could have it back. A package arrived a couple of days later in a thin unpadded envelope, full of broken glass slides and damaged audiotape. My heart sank, as did my view of British Council HQ staff.

Many years later I was at a lecture in the Royal Geographical Society in London, given by Alan Stimson, a former shipmate of mine, now retired from the National Maritime Museum at Greenwich. We enjoyed the lecture, and afterwards Alan introduced us to a friend who had worked abroad with the British Council. I expressed amazement at how such an incompetent lot in London could run such an excellent overseas operation. He said all British Council people overseas shared my view.

12. The Perfect Graduate

Does it annoy you sometimes to meet people who are so brilliant and perfect that they seem just too good to be true? We were interviewing for Blue Star Line Graduate Entry Scheme when a candidate came in front of us who had the best "A" level results I had ever seen and a top degree from a good university. My immediate thought was that he must spend all his time studying and would not make a practical seafarer. Further down his c.v. I found that he spent his vacations sailing and working in yachts and boats. Another stereotype came into my mind and I voiced my concern: "I expect your yachting consists of wearing smart clothes, wandering round the deck and putting the occasional fixes on the chart? What about real seamanship – the dirty work of maintenance and repair?" He replied "The Bosun and I always join two weeks early and overhaul all the rigging and gear ready for the trip!" There was no answer for it – he was perfect. When it came to consideration of his application, the panel thought there was no harm in offering him the job – but we doubted whether he would accept. The world was his oyster. To our surprise he accepted and did a couple of years before coming ashore to Imperial College in London, to do research into auxiliary wind power for commercial ships. He

was a very nice person. We stayed in touch for a while, but eventually his mathematical treatises were way over my head.

Many years later, our younger daughter Alison (seated in the picture) had been sailing with the Ocean Youth Club on the "Francis Drake" and here on the "Greater Manchester Challenge". I was talking to Colum Leggett, who had been mate on one of her trips. We were comparing notes on the various skippers and mates with whom we had sailed in coastal sailing craft. Colum said there was one Ocean Youth Club skipper who was better than all the rest. He organised the trips, encouraged and supported the crew members, mixed authority with delegation at just the right level etc – he was perfect! I asked if, by any chance, he was a former student of Imperial College. It was the same person! So not only was he perfect in navigation, seamanship, academic study etc, he was also a brilliant man manager! Wow!

13. General Studies

In the 1960s, the academic world was made aware that many college courses were very technical and narrow, producing young people who knew all about their area of work, but not much about life. This led to the inclusion of lectures labelled General Studies. Later, the same happened in schools where the General Certificate of Education Advanced Level in General Studies covered such wide subject areas that the examinations – many of which were multiple choice questions, were christened "multiple guess" by our children.

When I started teaching at the College of Technology, and had gained the highest nautical certificate, "Extra Master", I wanted to get further qualifications. Whilst waiting to see if I could do a Master's degree, I started a part time Higher National Diploma in Mathematics, Statistics and Computing at the College of Commerce. Most of the students were in their late teens having recently completed "A" levels and we had to attend General Studies with a lecturer from the college of commerce. Unlike my pre-sea course, where the non-technical lectures taught us the layout of docks and general hints on life at sea, our HND tutor seemed obsessed with deviance, crime and sex. Looking at the goings on in some inner cities in the year 2010, perhaps she did have the right idea in preparing us for life. At the time, however, from my personal point of view I thought the lessons were surplus to requirements, with one interesting exception.

One week we were given a long questionnaire to complete, which was all about our attitudes to life, money, community, welfare, crime, work etc. We filled in the answers and then were taught how to analyse the results. The purpose of the questionnaire was to objectively place us within the political spectrum from communism to fascism through all stations in between. For most people, the test worked. Those from the leafy suburbs came out somewhere amongst the ranks of conservatives and liberals, those from the poor areas where families had fierce loyalty to trades unions, came out in the socialist/labour party ranks. I was the exception. I came from leafy suburbs, but my attitude to life put me in heart of the socialists. I had to make all my classmates promise to keep this fact secret from the Conservative Party in Pensby, which I had recently joined. In the Wirral Peninsula, where we lived, the political colours went from bright red socialism in Birkenhead, westward to deepest blue conservatism in Heswall. Pensby was just west of the centre: maybe not pink, but definitely a lighter shade of blue.

14. Heavy Traffic in the Straits of Gibraltar

The real value of Radar Simulator courses, was that students could navigate through increasingly dense and difficult traffic in thick fog, and then go into the debriefing to explain to those on the other ships what they had done, and why they had done it. If they did collide, no ships were damaged and nobody killed. The picture shows Lecturer Charles Nicholls with a class of young officers.

In the early days of simulator courses, we had some very

experienced Masters and Senior Officers on the course. Most of them were from cargo and passenger liners, tankers, tramp ships or coasters. In trading ships there is always an urgency to complete loading, get to sea, get to the destination as soon as possible, discharge the cargo and load the next one. It was rush, rush, rush…..

We set up an exercise in thick fog in the Straits of Gibraltar with three ships abreast heading east into the Mediterranean and one heading west towards the Atlantic. The man in the westward bound ship was really worried and threaded his way carefully through the approaching group. In the de-briefing exercise he said "I would not have done that in real life!" We all asked what he would have done. He pointed to the chart and said "You see that little bay on the African coast? I would have gone down there and anchored, waited until the other ships had gone past and then come out to continue my voyage!" None of us could understand how a company could stay in business if their shipmasters went to "hide" when the traffic got a bit crowded. In chorus we asked "Which company are you from?" When we heard his answer, we understood. He was from the Meteorological Office Weather ships, which have to stay on station in the Atlantic to make meteorological observations and had no need to rush anywhere.

15. Seeing Through Brick Walls

Standing next to the scanner in the top room of the 1941 Harwich RDF (radar) Tower, I was reminded that the brick wall between me and the 15 miles of Harwich port approaches, was like a window to 50cm wavelength radio waves. Most radio waves travel through brick walls, or we would not be able to receive the BBC radio signals inside our houses. Camouflage for the radar tower was easy. No sign of scanners on the outside.

It reminded me of my good friend Willem Burger who taught ships' officers at the Radar School at Cardiff. When they had a new radar installed, they had a write-up in the local paper, which gave a few facts about radar, including the fact that radar waves pass through certain materials. That elicited an angry letter from an old lady who lived on the other side of Cardiff Bay, who was worried about all these seafarers looking into her bedroom when she was undressing. She need not have worried. No radar shows pictures in that much detail!

16. Mercury Motor Inn and Pilots

The United Kingdom maritime pilots were organised in two main groups, the UKPA (United Kingdom Pilots' Association) and the Transport and General Workers pilot section (the Union Pilots). I was told they would never sit down together and discuss the future of pilot training, but I was determined to try. It seemed like a good idea to get them away from the Polytechnic and City surroundings, so we organised the conference at the Mercury Motor Inn just outside Chester. The applications came in thick and fast. It turned out to be a very successful conference. We overflowed the Motor Inn and booked half the pilots into the Mollington Banastre Hotel, a couple of miles away.

On the second morning of the conference, a delegation of pilots complained "You have booked us into this Motor Inn and we are not happy at all. Did you see all those strange women in the bar last night. We think it is disgusting – almost like being in the red light district!" I apologised and said I would have a word with the management to see if there was anything we could do to improve the situation.

On the third morning of the conference I had another delegation of pilots coming to me complain. This time it was the group who were staying in the Mollington Banastre, which was very genteel and quiet. They said "We are not happy at all, being booked into the other hotel. If the pilots at the Mercury Motor Inn can have strange ladies in the bar in the evenings, why can't we?"

There is no pleasing some people!

17. The Acid Test

Hydrometer

When dealing with garages, standards of service depend very much on whether the staff they employ are properly trained and experienced. Like chefs and restaurants, if you find a good one, stick with it. Ann's father had been a garage owner before World War II, and when we were moving (with family and old Ford car) to Liverpool, he said "Blakes are the Ford agents there, and they always had a very good reputation." So I used Blakes. When I started teaching a yacht masters' class, I was surprised and pleased to find that one of my students, Norman Silk, was a director of Blakes. It always helps to know the boss! Blakes opened up a new outlet in Birkenhead and the foreman in the workshop looked after me very well.

One evening, I called to pick up my car after a service, and the foreman asked one of the young mechanics to explain exactly what work they had done. When he opened the bonnet, I noticed liquid on the top of the battery. I said "Looks as if it has been overfilled". He agreed with me, and went to get a hydrometer, opened the first cell, sucked out a quantity of acid, and proceeded to spray it into the air over me, the car and the surroundings. With some alarm, I shouted: "Hey, mind what you are doing, that is acid you are spraying!" As he opened the second cell to repeat the exercise he said "Its not acid. I ought to know, I put it in there. It is distilled water!" He just would not believe me, but as a concession to his fussy customer, sprayed the rest of the surplus acid on the floor.

He was quite right of course, what he had put into the battery earlier was distilled water. Unfortunately, he did not know that he was diluting acid, and when you mix two liquids, you cannot suck only one of them out again!

More From Research
and Consultancy

1. Interrogation and Perspectives

On my first visit to the British Ship Research Association at Wallsend on the River Tyne, I thought I had stumbled into the Gestapo headquarters. I was under intense interrogation in a small room, by a team of men led by George Snaith, senior manager of the BSRA. "We have heard some very disturbing stories about you!" they said "If they are true, we will not work with you – ever!" I asked what I had done. "It has come to our notice that you sometimes GIVE information away!" Innocently, I replied that, as a College Lecturer, that was what I was supposed to do. George took a deep breath and said "We are a research association – we SELL information. The Government has asked us to work with Liverpool Polytechnic, but if we do, you will have to sign a guarantee not to give anything away!"

There had been 25 bids for a Government contract to research into the use of computers on ships. Liverpool Polytechnic had bid with Decca Systems Study and Management Division against BSRA. When the Government chose, BSRA came first, our team were second.

The manager at Decca had said, as we were putting the bid together. "Remember, in funding bids, there are no prizes for coming second!"
However, in this case there were. The Government were impressed by the BSRA bid, which was mostly about building ships effectively, and our bid, which was about operating them efficiently. So they asked us to team up, which we did. The bridge between shipbuilders and ship operators is important.

Many years later as Master of the Honourable Company of Master Mariners, I was invited to speak at the Annual Dinner of the Royal Institution of Naval Architects. Expanding on the theme that people who design ships don't always consider those who sail in them, I said "The trouble with Naval Architects is that they think the end of the useful life of a ship is the day it is delivered new to the owners!" Their President, in his response said "That's great! We invite you to dinner, and you insult us! There are hundreds of Naval Architects in this room and – like me – they all know that what you said is untrue! We know that the end of the useful life of a ship is the end of the guarantee period!" They all laughed, but I think he had accepted my point.
The Nautical Institute set up a forum for designers and users to exchange information and feed back ideas. Whilst

I was President, with my counterparts in the Marine Engineering and Naval Architecture professional bodies, we tried to arrange for all ship designers to do at least one deep sea voyage before they designed ships. The best support we received was from Greek shipowners. In the UK, the owners were less enthusiastic – perhaps that tells us something.

2. Computers on Ships

My predecessor as Head of Nautical Studies at Liverpool Polytechnic was a clever and very far-sighted man. In about 1970, he sent members of staff off to do computer courses when most of us had never heard of computers and did not realise they would take over our lives. As a result of this far-sighted policy, I personally was able to do my Master of Philosophy 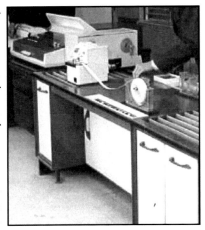 research degree running thousands of simulated voyages on an Elliott 803 computer programmed and provided with data by eight-hole punched paper tape.

It also meant that our research teams, working under the visionary direction of Keith Jones, were given Government contracts to look, amongst other things, at the use of computers in shipping. We joined up with a team from the British Ship Research Association (BSRA) in Tyneside and Decca Systems Study and Management Division in Surrey. First, we had to find out what computers would do, and then see whether the shipowners would buy and use them. Shipowners and seafarers were rightly suspicious of flashy salesmen. The salesmen were never on board when the new equipment let them down!

Visiting manufacturers you were confronted by the sales staff, who would tell you all the clever things their products would do, but would never admit that they had shortcomings. We were used to this with new radars and navigation systems. Computers were to be no different.

Having travelled round the country on a £250 "Thomas Gray Memorial Bursary" from the Royal Society of Arts while doing my research degree, I knew that every company had scientists doing real research who were only too pleased to meet equipment users and teachers and openly admit the problems and compromises in designing their equipment. I later told my students that these people were kept in a cage, and the "front office" managers would poke problems through the bars and then go back to collect the answers. They were never allowed to meet customers – they were too honest. It was a metaphorical cage, but a cage no less.

We should be eternally grateful for all the companies that let us into their back rooms to share ideas, Decca, Kelvin Hughes, Marconi, Hewlett Packard, Digital Equipment Corporation, AEI, the UK Hydrographic Office etc.
Next problem was to approach the shipowners. In order to do this, we had to draw up a list of companies operating

different classes of ships in different trades and then ask if we could conduct structured interviews with senior managers.

Interview with Bibby Line in Liverpool

Interviewing managers in Bibby Line, I took a keen research engineer from BSRA with me. He was hoping to implement links between computers on ships (a data highway) and linking it to the computers in Head Office. He asked "How many times an hour do you communicate with your ships?" The reply disappointed him. "Our Masters are in command of their own ships. They are the decision makers. They are on the spot. They know what is going on. Most of our masters report in once a week. We have one master who currently reports twice a week. We are not saying anything at present. We think he is a bit unsure of himself and needs moral support, so we let him call us!" The BRSA Engineer saw his fancy networks being redundant before they had even been born. Since those days we have seen the independence of the shipmaster slowly destroyed and more and more cases of decisions being taken by people ashore.

Interview at F T Everard and Sons in Greenhithe, Kent

F T Everard and Sons were operators of coastal ships and I was invited to talk to the senior member of the family who was in charge. He was friendly and helpful and interested in what we did at Liverpool Polytechnic, including the new BSc degree in which we would give future ship managers a blend of technical, financial, legal and commercial knowledge necessary to operate a ship or a shipping company.

I was well into the discussion of computers in navigation, engineering, communications and control systems, when the phone went. Mr Everard Senior apologised to me and then discussed the dimensions of a coaster with the caller. At the end of the conversation he said "OK! I will buy it!" Returning to the interview, we covered a few more questions and the phone went again. Again, dimensions were discussed and he said "OK! I will buy it!"

We were near the end of the interview when the phone rang again. Yet again the dimensions of a coaster were discussed, but the answer was different. "Well, I would like to buy it, but I have already bought two ships this afternoon. Before I buy a third one, I think I had better ask Aunty Ethel"

FOOTNOTE
When I was at school, "Ethel Everard" to me was a Thames Barge! The name was familiar, but I did not know the person after whom it was named.

Talking to Michael Everard in 2008, I understand the real and redoubtable Aunty Ethel was still alive and taking an interest in company affairs. A remarkable lady and a famous name.

3. Research for the National Ports Council

Keith Jones and I were doing research on getting ships in and out of port more quickly. The three ports chosen were the River Mersey, Harwich / Felixstowe and the River Tees. We plotted some nice graphs for passage times on the River Tees.

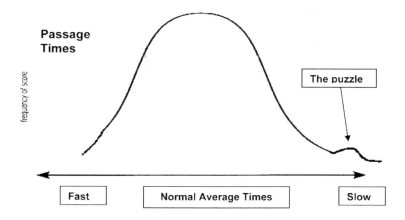

A few ships made fast passages, most made the passage from port entry to berth or vice versa in average times and a few were slow or very slow. Looking into the reasons for fast or slow passages, we found it depended on the size of the ships, the particular berth, ebb or flood tide, traffic density, waiting for tugs or mooring boats, weather and visibility, etc. All easy to understand.

There was a puzzling group of slow arrivals, for which we struggled to find a reason. They were all passages by the Shell tankers "Darina" and "Drupa." These were well-equipped manoeuvrable ships, they had very experienced officers and were regular visitors to the port. The lateness did not relate to any of the usual causes.

We had to ask the pilots and the Masters and officers of the ships. Shell had decided to fit the ships with very accurate "doppler" speed logs, which sent ultra-sound pulses to the seabed and measured the returns. The log had a big display on the bridge giving the speed in knots.

For years they had watched the banks of the river and looked over the side to judge speed. Now, as they approached each critical point in the passage, they had a big display telling them an exact number such as **"5.4 KNOTS"**. The numbers sounded too big, so they slowed down and arrived late.

Moral to this story is that numbers are just a way of describing things. They mean nothing unless you can relate them to real life!

4. Doppler Logs

When Shell were deciding which Doppler Logs to fit in their ships, they fitted one in a ship operating around the UK and Northern Europe, to see whether it lived up to claims in the manufacturer's glossy brochures. Reports coming back from the ship seemed to indicate that it was everything that they claimed, accurate, reliable, trouble-free. After several ships had been fitted, complaints started to come in saying that they did not work very well, were not accurate and gave quite a lot of trouble.

Going back to the Master of the ship on which the prototype was tested, the Marine Superintendent told his tale of woe and listed the complaints. The Master said "I am not surprised, we had a lot of problems too!"

"Wait a minute" said the Superintendent "Your report said it was great and did not give any problems. Why didn't you tell us the truth."

The Master "We did not want to disappoint you. We knew you had done a lot of research trying to find us a good speed log, and you would have been very disappointed if the results of your hard work turned out to be useless, so we gave it a good report!"

5. IMO Model Courses

When Bill O'Neil became Secretary General of the International Maritime Organization, he initiated several projects to evaluate its effectiveness. IMO had spent $2million donated by the Government of Norway, to create a framework of Model Courses to help developing countries raise the standard of their seafarer training. Had the money been spent wisely and was the project a success? IMO employed TecnEcon Transport Consultants to carry out an evaluation and I was part of the team.   By and large the Model Courses were effective but one or two interesting stories emerged.

A team from Norway took a course on search and rescue to West Africa. One of the tutors said the school in Ghana was near a beach on which a few wooden boats were drawn up. The equipment at the school was very basic.

They had only one bulb for their overhead projector, and worried they might have to stop short if the bulb blew. The Norwegians showed a film about search and rescue in the North Sea. There were flares, searchlights, aircraft, lifeboats, rescue helicopters and high-speed craft rushing around – very impressive! At the course evaluation one of the Ghanaians was asked what he thought of the film. "Very good!" he said "But I preferred Star Wars!"

Another Norwegian team went to China to try out a course about Liquefied Natural Gas Ships. They realised the part of the course about health issues would be useless if it used material filmed in Norway, so they asked their hosts to find a Chinese doctor to do that lecture and relate it to hospital facilities in China. A distinguished Chinese doctor agreed and asked if he could show a video as part of his presentation. Surprised, the team agreed! The doctor came in and showed his video. It was about heart transplants in California. The doctor said "Thank you for inviting me. Was that alright?" They said "That was a very impressive video, but it did not say anything about health issues on LNG ships." "Ah" said the doctor "I see you do not understand Chinese teaching! In China we lecture to impress the students with our knowledge, not to inform them. If we told them all the things we know, they would no longer respect us. We do not pass on our knowledge until we are on our deathbeds."

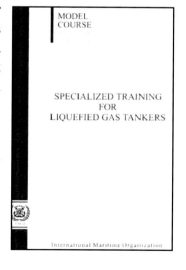

MODEL COURSE

SPECIALIZED TRAINING FOR LIQUEFIED GAS TANKERS

International Maritime Organization

Back at Liverpool Polytechnic I told this story at lunchtime in the staff refectory. I said to some physics lecturers "I cannot imagine teaching without passing on my knowledge." They replied "That may be so in Maritime Studies, but I don't think it is in the Physics Department!"

6. Fog or Gales?

Keith Jones and I were doing research for the National Ports Council on getting ships in and out of port more quickly. They wanted us to tell them that poor visibility was the problem and fitting bigger and better shore-based port radars was the answer. We told them that the problem was more likely to be associated with high winds and strangely, ships actually went in and out much more quickly in strong crosswinds – they had to or they would blow ashore. The real, problem was the damage they did because they were difficult to handle.

As a consultant, if you give your client the truth rather than the answer they want to hear, you get the sack. So we were sacked.

Wind is still a factor in the 21st Century:

High winds close container port

High winds in the North Sea closed a major container port for several hours on Tuesday afternoon.

Quayside cranes at the Port of Felixstowe in Suffolk were unable to work and available space for lorries filled up, a police spokeswoman said.

Cranes could not operate at the Port of Felixstowe

7. The Chamber of Shipping of the United Kingdom

The shipowners' organisations do a wonderful job today, with useful and relevant information and activities, as their website shows:

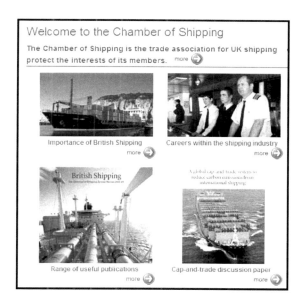

During the 1970s, my experiences were rather different. Liverpool Polytechnic won a contract from the Computer Systems and Electronics Division of the Department of Industry, to look into the future use of computers on ships. As project leader, I thought the fount of all wisdom would be the United Kingdom Chamber of Shipping in London, so I went to consult them. I knew they advised shipowners on all the latest radars and navigation systems, so thought they must have top-rate researchers evaluating each new product. When I asked how many graduates they had working for them, the polite retired RN Captain at the heart of the advisory service thought for a long time and then replied "None! We have no bright boys here!" All they did was to receive the publicity material from the electronics companies and send them on to their members. At least that meant that a bit of objective evaluation in Liverpool would not be duplicating what went on in London.

8. Live From the Bay of Biscay

Some of you may be old enough to remember the desktop computers for schools called the BBC Model B, introduced in 1982 by Acorn Computers. Keith Jones's team at Liverpool Polytechnic were given research funds for a two-year project to show how computers on ships could be linked over satellite to computers ashore. We expected to write long reports on the technical problems we encountered, but the Model B's were wonderful – very reliable and efficient. In the technical project, Mark Bradshaw was the key player, but he moved on to Silicon Valley in the United States to start his own company. We needed another leader for the next project.

The main interest in the research became the content of the messages rather than the technical feasibility, and Bernard Thomas was invited to take the lead. With colleague Tim Whalley, Bernie became the expert in exchanging information with ships and their company Information Management Consultants became a world leader. But that was in the future. First, we had to find out what ships wanted to know and what they wanted to tell people ashore. With the help of P&O and Cunard Line, Shell and a few other companies, we set up a system of electronic "pigeon holes" at the Polytechnic, where ships would place questions by 9 am each morning and could collect the answers at 5 pm the same day. The system was very popular with passenger ships and they would want the latest world and national news, sports results, stock exchange prices and other information, which was easily obtained ashore. As the service expanded to Europe the USA and South Africa, the information was sent in English, German, French and Spanish. If you go on a cruise in 2009 the chances are you will be provided each day with a special newspaper from Headland Media, who are the successors to IMC.

When the project was well underway, we were invited to the Chamber of Shipping in London to show the world our wonderful work. Having been caught out when equipment did not work in the past, I suggested that Bernie should have a "Plan B" in case his live link-up with a cable ship in the Bay of Biscay did not go to plan. Bernie was so confident, he decided to do it without a "safety net". In the middle of his talk he switched through the satellite to communicate with the ship and it all worked perfectly.

Throughout the presentation I had my fingers crossed and everything else as well. I was so relieved that it went well, but asked Bernie not to put me through such torture next time.

As I walked to the lift with senior members of the Chamber of Shipping hierarchy, one of them turned to me and said "Very impressive, but we know that you did not really talk to a ship, you had someone on a terminal in the room next door!" I was speechless. Bravery is not always recognised and rewarded!

9. Pressing the Buttons

I attended a meeting held on the first floor of the Chamber of Shipping headquarters in London to discuss some of the problems associated with the introduction of new technology in ships of the merchant fleet. Some of the experienced shipmasters present were very cautious about anything new – they had been caught before.

The most confident and enthusiastic person in the room was a recently-retired Royal Navy Captain who offered his help. "I have just been in command of the Royal Navy's latest guided missile destroyer. If you want to know anything about new technology, I am your man!"

At the end of the meeting he was first to get to the lift. He looked at the two buttons and said "Which button do you press to go down? I never know which one!" Someone behind me whispered "That is the trouble with Royal Navy officers, they are used to having someone else press the buttons for them!"

In the Merchant Navy we have to press our own.

10. The Best New Gyro Compass

Life at sea is a well-ordered existence where everyone knows their place and just gets on with their work. It was the same in the Maritime Studies Department of Liverpool Polytechnic. Other departments thought it was strange that our students in the good old days called the lecturers "Sir."

Former seafarers entering the rat race of shore employment often did not understand the devious and underhand tactics that people use to survive. Newly appointed shore-based Marine Superintendents relied heavily on their older and more experienced counterparts for advice. One such told me that his first job was to recommend new gyrocompasses for a series of six new tankers. There had been several changes in design and operation of gyro compasses and he did not know which was best. He knew his opposite number in a rival tanker company had just supervised the building of new ships and asked him "Which gyro compasses did you fit?" He though he could not go far wrong if he recommended the same for his ships, which he did. The compasses were unreliable and costly to maintain – a really bad batch. A few months later at a Chamber of Shipping meeting he met his opposite number and said "You know those gyros you recommended. We fitted them and they have been nothing but trouble!"
The older and wiser one replied "We had terrible problems with ours, too!"
The younger one: "If you knew that, why did you recommend them?"

Reply, "I didn't recommend them. You asked what we had fitted and I told you!"

Moral to that story, is ask the right question.

11. Radar Scanners and Sheep

Most ships' radar scanners consist of a metal slotted waveguide enclosed in a fibreglass cover. The fibreglass is transparent to radar waves so they do not affect the radar transmissions or returning echoes. If coated in salt water spray, the cover reflects or absorbs the signals. To let the radar user know the radar has lost power, a transmission sensor is placed nearby and lights up on the display when transmission strength falls.

Former Polytechnic lecturer Alan Bole is a well known expert on radar. Off-shore rigs were placed in the Irish Sea and it was decided to place the scanner on a Welsh hill to monitor passing traffic. Alan was the consultant. They told him that, as there was no sea spray on the mountain, they were going to save money by dispensing with the transmission monitor.

After a while the quality of the radar displays deteriorated rapidly. It looked as if the transmitter was to blame. The culprit was a Welsh farmer. Like many people (including some W.R.N.S. girls sadly misled in World War II) he had heard that radar waves make men sterile. He was putting his rams out with the ewes near the scanner, and he was not going to have his rams made sterile. In a fit of anger, he peppered the scanner with his shot-gun. The cover was

damaged and rain did the rest. I understand that after the repair, it was thought that it might, after all, be a good idea to fit a transmission monitor, even on a Welsh hill.
Thanks to Alan for this story.

12. Philippine Potholes

Strange things have been happening to the weather in recent years. As far as Manila in the Philippines is concerned, that has meant a lot more rain, because the Inter-Tropical Convergence Zone has come further north and stayed over the country for much longer than usual. Strange things also happen in local politics. The City Councillors are alleged to get a "back-hander" from the road contractors. If the roads had been repaired properly, this would be a one-off payment. But if they are repaired badly, the exercise has to be repeated each year, much to the satisfaction of the councillors and contractors. The population, however, is not so happy, because they have to cope with large potholes in the road.

I had been with Videotel's agent meeting shipping company and crew manning agency clients. As the time grew near for me to depart, the heavens opened in a deluge. A kind shipping company manager said "You will never get to the airport in an ordinary car or taxi. I have a 4X4. I will take you!"

As we navigated through floods and potholes, he said to me "The real danger here is the medium size potholes!" I said "Surely you mean the really big ones?" "No!" he said "You can see the tops of the buses in those!"

We made it, and I was very grateful for his help.

13. Philippine Traffic and Transport

At a busy meeting in a shipping company's first floor office in Manila, there was a gentle knock at the door and a very polite secretary asked my colleague Kjell Sundberg "Did you come by car?" He said "Yes!" She advised us to look out of the window. Sure enough, a police tow-truck was just lifting the front of our car into a towing position and was about to drive off with it – with my luggage in the boot.

Kjell had told me earlier that one of the people in his office had had an interesting experience with the police and army. He had reported his car stolen. Rumour had it that the police/army were exporting stolen cars, so he might never see it again. A few weeks later they rang him up and said "First the good news! We have found your car! Second, the bad news! It is being used by a senior army officer and he rather likes it, so you can't have it back yet!" He was advised that he could insist on having it back, but it might put his life in danger. So he waited. Eventually they rang up and said he could have it back, but by then it was damaged and stripped and worth nothing, so he claimed on his insurance for a replacement.

Getting back to our car. Kjell and I rushed down to the street. While I struggled to retrieve my luggage from the boot, he bravely placed himself in a position where they would have to run him over to get away. In the event they only asked for a very high fine, drove round the block with the car, and put it back in the same parking spot. Kjell had taken the precaution of hiring a driver with the car, and had told him not to park it anywhere where it might be towed away. The driver said "I was only away a few minutes, I had to go to the toilet!" He did not receive any bonus for that day!

14. A Testing Time

There is a lot of debate in the UK about testing in schools these days. Some people say it detracts from teaching time, and leads teachers to limit their lessons to the topics that will be examined. I have not joined the debate, but I do have a little voice in my head from one of my mentors as a teacher, Keith Jones who said, "If you cannot measure the difference between the student's performance at the beginning and end of the course, you do not know how effective your teaching has been."

With this in mind, my presentations at the World Maritime University in Sweden normally ended with a test. In recent years I chose a Case Study in which two ships had collided in the China Sea. The officers each saw the other ship, identified it with the wonderful new Automatic Identification System, called it up on the VHF radio, and discussed who should alter course or slow down (they disagreed about which rule applied). They were still debating the point when their ships collided, fortunately a glancing blow, but a salutary lesson in when to use common sense and take drastic early action and when to use the technology in a prolonged debate. Having briefed the WMU students and stepped them through the situation leading up to the encounter, I asked the 32 young people from all over the world, what action they would have taken. Perhaps I should not have been surprised when 94% would have chosen to "Identify the other ship with AIS and talk on the VHF radio". They would have had the collision! We give young people new technology, and they think we want them to use it.

118

I repeated the Case Study during presentations in Hong Kong, Sydney Australia and Auckland, New Zealand. The further East I went, the older the audience and the fewer people would have been duped by the new technology. One shipmaster in Auckland said "To hell with these new fangled devices, I would go hard a-starboard and get out of there!"

An unexpected outcome of these presentations was that I accidentally tested the Chief Government Marine Advisor to the Hong Kong Government and the Master of the new Cunard liner "Queen Victoria" who was waiting to take command when the ship arrived in Sydney on her maiden voyage. Both passed, and both were generous in their acknowledgement of the lessons I was trying to get across, and encouraged me to keep doing it!.

15. Everard's and P&O

During my school days and sea career, the two companies F.T. Everard and Sons of Greenhithe and the Peninsula and Oriental Steam Navigation Company of London were at two ends of the spectrum of shipowning in England. P&O were very grand and proud. Everards just got on with the job of operating smaller ships around the coast and continent without pomp and ceremony.

Such were the fortunes of British shipping in the late 20th Century, that Everards became one of the major British companies, and the Everard family, with its vast experience of running ships in a very competitive marketplace, gave their knowledge and support to managers of bigger companies which were struggling a bit. This brought together in the General Council of British Shipping (the shipowners' organisation) Michael Everard and Lord Sterling of P&O.

During a period of corporate munificence in 1976 P&O had bought the former Everard Thames Sailing Barge "Will Everard," which had been renamed "Will." P&O had refurbished it for corporate hospitality and made good use of it entertaining clients and potential clients.

| Offered on the Internet |
| Ship Kit of |
| "Will Everard" or "Will" |
| by Billing Boats |

In a speech at a formal shipowners' dinner, Lord Sterling of P&O aimed a "barb" at their "lowly" associates by asking Michael Everard to describe the differences between their two companies. Michael in his response had exactly the right reply. "Whatever the differences between our two companies, I can assure you all of one thing. Everards have never bought second hand ships from P&O!" Nice one!

16. "It's Huge!"

It was a very rainy day in Glasgow as I walked through the revolving door of the shiny new offices of the old established shipping company J J Denholm. There was a walk of several yards from the door to the reception desk, behind which were two smart lady receptionists. When I was about half way to the desk, the two ladies leapt to their feet, pointed towards my lower half and screamed loudly in unison "Och!! It's Huge!!" Nonplussed for a moment, I slowly looked down and I had to agree with them, it was huge – a massive spider walking with me.

I picked it up, took it to the door, and in one revolution threw it out into the rain. In another revolution it was back inside. The next time, I took it outside, walked down the street and put it into the doorway of the next office. When I returned, I enjoyed the sort of reception that St George must have had when he had slayed the dragon.

17. Taint

In Blue Funnel Line general cargo ships, which carried a variety of spices and primary products from the Far East, some cargoes were very sensitive to taint from the smell of others. Nobody would want to buy tea that smells of rubber, or tapioca that smells of palm oil. The different cargoes had to be stowed well away from one another, in different hatches, different compartments or at least ventilated with the smelly cargo "down wind" from the sensitive stuff.

When helping Blue Star Line with the interviewing of graduate entrants, I learned that the sensitivity of chilled and frozen cargoes was event more critical. On one occasion a large consignment of lamb was stowed near enough to another commodity, oranges, for the whole consignment of meat to be ruined. The company was about to destroy all the tainted lamb, when some clever person came up with an idea.

The company bought some of the oranges and sent them to the butchers' shops they owned, with the lamb. The shops were told to give customers two free oranges with each joint of lamb. If the customers came back and complained that the lamb tasted of oranges, they were to be asked; "Did you get free oranges?" If the answer was "Yes", the next question was "And did you carry them home in the same shopping bag as the lamb?" If the answer was "Yes" again, the reply was "Well, there you are then!" Problem solved.

More Holidays and Travel

1. Hitch Hikers

When driving all over the country in the 1950s and 60s I quite often picked up hitchhikers. On a long journey it was nice to meet someone new and talking made the journey seem shorter. I shall only mention two.

Driving from London to Dovercourt in Essex, I stopped to pick up a young man on the A12 on the outskirts of London. He was a soldier from a unit in Devon on an initiative test. He asked me to drop him off in Colchester. He said they had been sent off in pairs on Friday afternoon with no money and had to return on Monday morning with the answer to a question. In their case the question was how many gallons of paint it takes to paint the Forth Bridge in Scotland. I asked why he wanted to go to Colchester. He said "Because I live there!" His colleague lived in Edinburgh and would find out the answer to the question and he would enjoy a weekend at home. I said, "Weren't you supposed to stay together?"

"Yes" he replied "But it is an INITIATIVE test!"

The second time, I was heading from Liverpool to Harwich and in gloomy light saw two bedraggled people wanting a lift. I took pity on them. When the couple got in the car I realised from the aroma and the scratching that they were not going to be ideal travelling companions. Their conversation was not exactly sparkling either. I hoped they were not going far. Unfortunately they were – all the way to Essex.

After that experience and in the light of stories about robbers and highjackers, I don't pick up hitchhikers any more – a pity really.

2. Montreal Metro and Chicago South Bend Railroad

Visiting Canada and the Great Lakes for the first time on the "Manchester Port", I had plenty of advice from the Manchester Liners personnel for whom it was a second home. The first bit of advice concerned the underground, the Montreal Metro. They told me that as soon as I boarded the train, I should grab hold of something and quickly sit down. They were not wrong. The metro is brilliant. It runs in a trough on rubber wheels and is very fast. The stations are built at higher level than the main track, and as soon as the train leaves the station, it "falls off" and whizzes down to the lower level. Just before the next stop it climbs a steep slope and rapidly decelerates. If you do not hang on, you finish in a heap, at the end of the carriage. Sound advice: get on, hold on, sit down!

Chicago today is a modern city. Back in 1968 it was different. At the opposite end of the spectrum of railway history from Montreal Metro was the South Shore and South Bend Railroad. It ran close to Calumet Harbour, where the ship was berthed. There were no stations. The huge locomotive with a cow-catcher on the front would come steaming down the track and anyone wishing to board would hold up their hand to stop it and climb aboard. I was told that British people were hopeless because they would timidly put their hand half way up when the train was almost past. The driver, if he saw them, would slam the brakes on and the train would screech to a halt, depositing the unwary passengers at the front end of each carriage. You then had to creep aboard to join a very hostile group of bruised fellow passengers. Sound advice again: Signal early, hand held up high and look really determined to stop the train!

3. Anyone for the boat?

Some railways ran express trains that connected with ferry services. These were often referred to as "boat trains". Although not designated as such, some of the early evening trains from London to Liverpool carried passengers getting the night boat from Liverpool to Belfast. If the train was delayed, the guard would go through the train asking "Anyone for the boat?" and telephone ahead to delay sailing to wait for them.

On one occasion the train from London had been stuck on the viaduct over the Weaver Navigation Canal, near Northwich for nearly an hour. As passengers, we could see the small ships passing underneath. I was sitting next to a large family of Irish people, parents and several children. The guard came through saying "Anyone for the boat?" The Irish family looked out of the window at a small coaster passing below, and said to the guard. "No thank you, I think we will stay on the train!"

4. A Cure for Road Rage

Travelling along a narrow lane in North Wales, we were behind a minibus which was indicating that it wanted to turn right. Way before the junction, it pulled over to the right hand side of the road, to be confronted by a large car coming quite fast round the corner, meeting it head-on. They stopped dead – bumper to bumper. The car driver was a big man, red face and very  angry!! He leapt out and advanced on the minibus, his face getting redder and redder and his arms flailing, as he marched forward. As he pulled back the door of the minibus, there was an immediate change in his demeanour, the anger shrank back inside and he looked as if he might implode rather than explode! The bus was full of nuns!

5. Steam and Trains

Travelling home to Dovercourt, Essex on steam trains, after a long voyage always seemed to take ages. Not helped on this occasion because the line from Liverpool to Crewe was blocked for some reason and we were advised to travel via Warrington. This involved getting a Manchester train to Warrington Central, then a local train to Warrington Bank Quay where you could get on a Glasgow train bound for London. Arriving at Central, it was announced that the local train to Bank Quay was about to depart. I rushed to the local train with all my luggage It was very crowded, with people standing in every carriage – except one – which was empty. I grabbed the door handle, opened the door and threw my bags in. I noticed immediately that it was a bit damp. I slammed the door and the train moved out right away. As soon as the locomotive started to pull away, a hissing sound in the corner of the carriage announced the broken steam heating pipe. The carriage filled with steam. We crept round the tight curve at snails pace and then stopped for ages waiting to join the main West Coast Line. There was no corridor, so I remained in my steam oven, getting hotter and wetter. Eventually we pulled into the station and I was able to escape. Moral to this story: If you feel very lucky to find an empty seat, check before taking it.

Recently Warrington Bank Quay has been in the news after "no kissing" signs appeared following concerns that embracing couples were causing congestion.

With Wirral Choral Society, singing at an old folks home, one of the basses (not me!) arrived late and was surprised to find a vacant seat in the front row. He sat in it and we started singing. He discovered when he stood up, that his luck was not as good as he thought, but his trousers dried out quite quickly. Same moral!

6. Leonardo impressions

HQS "Wellington" is moored at Temple Stairs on Victoria Embankment – busy road, busy pavement. Security is an important issue. I was surprised as I arrive to board the ship, to see a young man right in the bow of the ship, leaning over in the manner of Leonardo DiCaprio in the film "Titanic."
Standing by the gangway was his friend.
Our conversation went as follows:

Me: "What is he doing?"

Him: "E's enjoyin' 'is self!"

Me: "Oh! Is he!"

Him: "D'you fink 'eed better git orf!"

Me: "Yes. I think he had better get off!"

Him, shouting loudly to "Leonardo": "Git Orff!! You've outstayed your welcome!"

As they walked off along the Embankment, I gave some thought to improving security on the ship.

7. London's Cabbies

The taxi drivers of London are a special breed. They recently formed their own Livery Company, The Worshipful Company of Hackney Carriage Drivers. They are proud of their knowledge of the city and are generous with their time and money when it comes to taking poor children on outings. Their charitable efforts are supported by other Livery Companies too.

During my year as Master of the Master Mariners, they had their offices aboard our Headquarters Ship "Wellington". I was to discover, that no matter how well they learn "The Knowledge" when they are young, as they get old they forget…

My Letter to the Chairman, The Company of Hackney Carriage Drivers:

Last weekend we had 530 visitors to the "Wellington" and I explained how, in the Middle Ages the boatmen on the Thames would take passengers half way across and then double the fare or invite the passengers to get off in mid stream. The Watermen's Company was set up to regulate the standards. Likewise through history, the other Livery Companies set standards of products and services for the City. I told them that unlicensed cabs today are much the same as those 13th century boatmen. You do not know where they will take you or how much it will cost. Recently, I was in Copenhagen where most of the taxis are driven by illegal immigrants from former Yugoslavia, they

132

don't speak Danish or English, don't know the city and charge extortionate fares. I explained how lucky we are to have properly trained Hackney Carriage Drivers with "the knowledge".

Today, I was due to have lunch with the Painters' Company in Little Trinity Lane. Two taxi drivers did not know where it was, worse still, two thought they knew and sent me towards Trinity Square. I was very embarrassed and finally arrived late with my wife "remote piloting" the taxi from an A-Z of London in our flat, by mobile telephone. Please will you make sure all future drivers can find the Livery Halls!!!!

Sorry I missed the send-off for Disneyland Paris. My wife and I are moving house at present and we were getting to the critical part of the contract exchanges.

I thought you would be interested in the above story.

8. The Strand Palace and Savoy Hotels

133

In 1976, on the 50th Anniversary of the founding of the Honourable Company of Master Mariners, a cocktail party was to be held on board the Headquarters Ship "Wellington," with the Queen and the Duke of Edinburgh as guests of honour.

The day of the party was sunny and very hot and I was working in London all day. Ann was travelling down to meet me. We needed somewhere to shower and change. I rang the Strand Palace Hotel and said "My wife and I need a room for about an hour this afternoon, is that possible?" The receptionist seemed a bit suspicious or at least cautious. "Well!" she said "The manager has told me about people like you. He says it will be alright, but you will have to pay the full night rate!" Overhearing the conversation, Ann's mother said "Don't go to the Strand Palace, ask the Savoy Hotel, and I will pay!"

We rang the Savoy, they asked no questions, gave us a room with a marble bathroom and load of clean towels, and charged £15. What excellent service.

9. Edinburgh and Aberdeen

The annual meetings of the Association of Navigation Schools took place in summer and were usually a good day out – well, three days out, in fact. In 1978 the association combined the annual meeting with the opening, by Prince Charles, of the brand new campus of Leith Nautical College. Ann and I enjoyed the visit.

A few years later, I was on another Association visit to the College, without Ann. After a day of meetings, I went to the bus stop, to travel back to Edinburgh and catch the train home. Several other college principals were also at the stop and got on the bus before me. On boarding, I realised that there was a cylinder that required the exact fare, and I had five-pound notes, but no change. I walked down the bus and asked the people I recognised if they had any change. They lent me the money and I paid the fare.

As the bus pulled away, a woman sitting behind me said quite loudly in my ear "You are lucky this is Edinburgh and not Aberdeen! My daughter went out without her purse in Aberdeen and nobody there would give her the fare. She was waiting at the stop for ages!" I suddenly realised that she thought I had begged the fare from strangers.

Strangely, my friends from Aberdeen don't think this story is at all interesting or amusing. Edinburgh friends think it is an obvious truth.

10. France used to be a very civilised country

In 2008 the new French President has announced that they are going to get rid of one of the most civilised of practices – the long lunch with good food and wine – usually lasting from 1230 until about 3 pm. That would be a pity.

Liverpool Polytechnic was part of a group that organised the early series of symposia on "Vessel Traffic Services", the organisation of shipping traffic from shore-based radar and communication centres. We were going to hold the next one in France, and had arranged a meeting in Paris to finalise the arrangements. There were no flights direct from Liverpool, so I stayed the night in Hertfordshire with Julian Parker, Secretary of the Nautical Institute, and we took the first flight from Heathrow to Paris. We arrived at about 9.45 am and the meeting had already started at 9.30. At coffee time I said to the French chairman "Can we start the next meeting at 10 am?" and he agreed.

As 1230 approached and items were being rushed through so we could finish on time, the chairman announced "The next meeting will start at 9.30 am on ………." I put up my hand and said "Excuse me, at coffee time you agreed to start the next meeting at 10 o'clock!" He said "Ah yes, but since then, I have been thinking. If we start at 9.30, two Englishmen miss two items on the agenda. If we start at 10 o'clock, all of us here (indicating the whole multinational

committee) will miss the first half hour of lunchtime – so we start at 9.30!"
What a civilised approach to life!

11. Caravan Holidays in Norway

Like Alaska, building roads along the coast was a major problem when opening up northern parts. With both, the sea became the first major highway to the north and the Norwegian Hurtigruten (Coastal Express) service is over a century old. It became the most important communication link between the north and south and it is from these pioneering voyages that the Hurtigruten tradition stems. Translating as 'fast route', it was the quickest and most reliable passage into the remote lands of northern Norway, regardless of weather conditions. Indeed it was not until 1983 that the mail delivery was finally entrusted to road and air routes. It is this heritage and experience that marks out Hurtigruten as one of the most professional and proficient expedition voyage operations on earth.

Whilst on the coastal express, we passed a Norwegian family towing a caravan. In the strong headwinds, it was not making much progress.

The roads to the north are now of very high standard and we were surprised to see a caravan being towed by a boat.

12. Norwegian pigeons

On the voyage to the north of Norway on the coastal steamer, we saw many examples of the local knitwear, with its typical Scandinavian patterns.

It was summer time as we walked through a park in Bergen, and there were some pigeons walking round our feet. On looking at them more closely, they looked as if the were wearing Scandinavian pullovers. Have a look at the pictures. What do you think?

13. Age

Travelling from Milton Keynes into London on a busy train, I was surprised and delighted when a young man offered to change seats, so that Ann and I could sit together. A woman opposite said to him "You are a real gentleman, Sir!. You don't often see real gentlemen these days!" I though he might even get a round of applause.

Having passed the age of 70, I have noticed that, having all my life given up my seat to ladies, particularly pregnant ones, the tide is now turning. Many times in the last two years young ladies (particularly Chinese young ladies) have offered me their seat on the underground. At first it made me feel very old, but more recently, I have come to appreciate Chinese philosophy, which encompasses respect for old age. I am all for it!

14. Mice and Messages

Have you noticed that it is almost obligatory to include misspellings and errors in emails and text messages? People are in such a rush they never seem to go back and check whether what they have written makes sense.

Ann and I overheard a telephone conversation between a man on the train and someone we presume was his brother. It went something like this:
"I have had an email message for you from Mum. She has asked me to remind you to take the mice out of the fridge to defrost in time for dinner.
I didn't know we ate mice, but you are the chef, so presumably you know what it is all about.
On second thoughts, if you can't find any mice, perhaps she meant mince."

More Cultural Exchanges

1. Bicycles, Junks and Demons

On one of my first visits to Penang, in Malaya, my Uncle Len, who was a harbour master, had picked me up from the ship and was driving me to his house for lunch. We drove through the crowded streets of Georgetown and out into the suburbs. We were overtaking an old Chinese man on a bicycle, and as we drew nearly level with his back wheel, he suddenly swerved across in front of the car. We missed him by a whisker. He quickly recovered his poise and gave us a smile and a friendly wave. Uncle Len did not flinch. He explained the Chinese superstition. Some Chinese people believe that everyone is followed by demons, and if you can get someone to cross very close behind you, they cut off the demons. It is a lucky thing to do.

Later in my career, when I was officer of the watch on Blue Funnel ships going up the coast of China, I often went through fleets of fishing junks. They usually made a space for the big ship to pass, but every so often, when a junk was going to pass very close down one side of the ship, at the last minute, it would alter course right under the bow. It would disappear, and later emerge from under the flare of the bow, abeam of number two hatch. The junk crew would give a friendly smile and wave as they passed. If I had not known about the demons, I would have been really worried.

Returning to Hong Kong in 2008, we found that the junks and sampans are motorised, but the superstitions are still in evidence amongst the people in them!

2. Visitors from Colombia

When the Nautical College in Bogota in Colombia, South America, bought a UK-built radar simulator, they needed a course on how to make the best use of it. Liverpool Polytechnic was asked to help. Two Colombians came to work with us. They arrived on the first evening of the Mersey River Festival which was opened with fireworks and aquatic displays. They enjoyed it – for a moment they thought it was all for them! One was a former Merchant Ship Captain, who spoke good English and was very "switched on. " He knew what he needed to learn. He was to be the leading Course Tutor in Bogota.

The second man was a former military electrician, who was to look after the setting up and maintenance. At first, we could not understand anything he said, but colleague Alan Bole cracked the problem. Whilst in the Colombian services, the electrician had been sent to a US base in Texas for training. Most of the people there ignored him, so he spent most of his time at the cinema, where his passion was cowboy films. Alan started to talk to him in "cowboy" language. For example, after work: "Say Pardner, shall we mosey down to the saloon for two ringers of rye...." etc Eyes lit up and the barrier was broken.

Later, we drove to the Simulator Manufacturer's factory in Surrey. We chose the Welsh border roads to show them the scenery. They were stunned by it. Looking at the green hills and valleys, the Captain, voice full of wonder, said "There is a special English word for this! What is it?"
Me: "Beautiful"
Him: "No!"
Me: "Picturesque"
Him: "No!"
Me: "Lovely"
Him: "No!"
Me: "Scenic"
Him: "No!"
Me: "Pretty"
Him: "No!"
Me: "Attractive"
Him: "No! There is a special word for it. Where did Alice go in the fairy story"
Me: "Wonderland!"
Him; "That is it – WONDERLAND!"

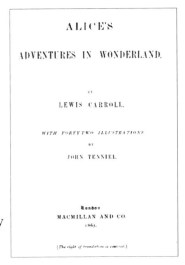

142

Since that time, whenever I see Welsh hills I am reminded of "Wonderland".

3. Scottish Pound Notes

Taking over as Director of the School of Engineering and Technology Management, I was expected to add to the excellent engineering courses, some business studies, management and economics, to equip our students, many of whom would work in small companies, to be effective as entrepreneurs, rather than just making better and better engineering "widgets" and failing to notice that their companies were going bust.

I was told at the last minute that a "Prof" from the Technical University in recently "liberated" Budapest, would be joining us to see how we did it. The "Prof" turned out to be Dr Edit Romvari. She told me that, under communism, everyone was told what to do, and did it, even if reluctantly. With "freedom" her pupils needed to be motivated to create their own businesses. She had our problem, only worse.

She had never been to the west before this visit, and had learned her English in the classroom. Her English was excellent. When we showed her round the historic and cultural sights of the northwest and north Wales, she used colloquial expressions and idioms that at first amazed us, and later we took for granted. She would use a phrase and then say to Ann or myself: "Did I get that right? I thought you would remark on it!"

Of all the incidents during her visit, one stood out. She wanted to visit Edinburgh, and went off one weekend. She really enjoyed the sights and history of the city. She had one awkward moment. Before she came to the UK, someone had warned her that, if she went to Scotland, she should not take Scottish pound notes back to England, as some shopkeepers were a bit "iffy" about taking them. Buying a souvenir, she was given Scottish pound notes in her change. She said; "Can I have coins instead, please?" The very indignant and angry shop assistant said: "What is the matter with Scottish pound notes?" Edit said she was taken aback, but thinking on her feet, she remembered walking past a phone box. She said: "I need to make a phone call and they won't go in the slots!" She got her coins. Honour saved all round. Quite a lady!

4. Can you give a lecture?

In 1986, on a busy day in Liverpool Polytechnic, I had a phone call from London. I was asked "Can you give a lecture on the use of new technology at sea?" I said I could. We discussed the overall scope of the conference, the time I would be allocated, the facilities, the date and time etc. As an afterthought, I said "Where am I going to be giving this lecture?" I was surprised to be told it was not London, but the Taj Mahal Hotel in Bombay!

Rajiv Ghandi was Prime Minister and was determined that his India would be a leader in technology by the turn of the century. His Government invited people from all over the world to explain what was needed. I was flown First Class by Air India from Heathrow to Bombay and back. (It was usually called Bombay then, rather than Mumbai as it is today)

Landing a 5 a.m., I came though customs with two other speakers who were attending the conference. There were three cars waiting for us. I suggested that we should all go in one car and let the other drivers have some time off. That was not allowed, as the two who were not needed, had to be employed. So we travelled into the city in convoy! A lot of very poor people were sleeping on the pavements and in large drainage pipes which were ready to be laid. Their bed spaces were marked out with chalk on the paving stones, and rats were running round them. A bit of a culture shock for Westerners.

When the conference opened, I sat in the front row and chatted to the important-looking gentleman sitting next to me. He said he was "The D.G.." I discovered he was responsible for the Indian Government's shipping and ports policy – a very important job. I asked what he hoped would come out of the conference. He said he was just there to listen. He actually knew nothing about shipping. In the Indian Civil Service, (modelled on the worst aspects of the UK's?) when you are due for promotion, you are promoted to the next job at the higher rank. If you were in charge of hospitals and the next job was in shipping, off you go, and manage as best you can!

Several UK lecturers were there including Professor Couper from the University of Wales Cardiff. I was very lucky with the timing of my lecture. A Professor from East Germany followed me. He covered the same topics as me, but because he was after me, it

146

looked as if he was copying! If I had been second, I would have appeared to be the one with no ideas of my own!

When I got home, I met Mr **C**.P. Srivastava, the Secretary General of the International Maritime Organization (the United Nations Agency for shipping). I thought he would be interested in my trip. I discovered he had arranged it!

NOTE: Talking to members of the Physics Department at the Polytechnic about the waste of manpower and resources in India by using three cars and three drivers when one was adequate, I was surprised when one of the lecturers said "I think it is a very sensible idea. What would have happened if the one car broke down!" That is the trouble with academics. They have no idea about running a profitable business in the real world. I wonder if they would send their transport round in threes in case one broke down.

5. Prime Ministers

Two to Watch

Anyone who lives in the constituency which has the Speaker of the House of Commons as their Member of Parliament may think they are disenfranchised because the Speaker does not vote. In the Wirral constituency we had Selwyn Lloyd as our MP when he was Speaker. He was returned unopposed so there was no canvassing to do, but there was time

for long relaxed chats with him. He told us we should not worry about local issues being ignored. He could get things done behind the scenes because he knew just the right people to ask if something needed to be done. He also told us that there were two young women we should watch. They had both been recently elected to parliament, and were feisty and intelligent and were going places. In the Conservatives it was Margaret Thatcher and in the Labour Party, Barbara Castle. Having been alerted, we followed their fortunes as they progressed. Mrs Thatcher was very successful, as we all know. My theory is that this was because many of the Tory MPs had been under the thumb of their nannies or their matron at public boarding schools. Barbara Castle was in the Labour Party where all men were created equal but that didn't include the women who should be at home cooking while they were in the Working Men's Club. Poor Barbara never made it to Prime Minister.

Edward Heath

At the time when we were teaching a Yachtmasters Evening Class at the Polytechnic, several of us would usually go to the Boat Show at Earls Court in London each January. It was a bit depressing because the boats on show cost much more than we could ever afford and we would end up with a pile of brochures about radars and navigation systems and an odd accessory or two, like a shackle or a bottle screw, or a book about sailing or rule of the road at sea. Coming down a stairway and swinging round the pole at the bottom, I bumped into someone I recognised instantly, but I was very surprised that it was not mutual recognition – he stared straight through me. Then I realised it was Edward Heath, the Prime Minister. I recognised him from the TV. The trouble with television is that the celebrities cannot see the viewers!!

Harold Wilson

The North of England Education Conference, held in the Adelphi Hotel In Liverpool each year, attracted teachers from all over the north of England including me. Harold Wilson, Labour MP for Huyton on Merseyside, also attended and we found ourselves in the foyer during a coffee break and had a chat. His opening gambit was to put his finger under his tie and say "I bet you don't know what this organisation is!" I looked and said "I do! It is the tie of Trinity House, the pilotage and lighthouse authority!" He went on to say that he and Winston Churchill both wore Trinity House ties. He was proud to have been a junior assistant to Churchill in Italy at the end of World War II. We talked about putting jokes into speeches. He said Harold Macmillan had told him that two jokes were fine, but you should be very careful, three or more turned

a serious speech into a comedy show. Perhaps that is why my lectures were not always taken seriously.

Looking back at his time as Prime Minister, he said his greatest achievement was the founding of the Open University.

He was very proud of its success and said that his son, who was a lecturer at Oxford, used texts from the OU as they were better than anything he could find in his University.

Later, I shared a Videotel office in London with Lord Walter Perry of Walton, the first Vice Chancellor of the Open University. Walter told me that Harold Wilson had asked him to set up the Open University in such a way that an incoming Conservative Government could not shut it all down again. He had a maximum of three years before the next election – a mammoth task. Reading the history books I find that not all the Labour Party were keen to keep the OU either. Walter worked away for a year, when the Prime Minister again approached him. "Bad news, I am afraid! The party is losing ground in the opinion polls so I am going to the country a year early! So Walter had only the balance of two years to make the OU "watertight". The success of the Open University today is evidence that he made it.

Sri Lanka

I was on a round-the-world tour as President of the Nautical Institute in the 1990s. We were presenting papers on safety and accident prevention to local audiences, with the help of local Nautical Institute branches in Vancouver, Hong Kong, Colombo and Dubai. We were made welcome everywhere, but in Sri Lanka the Prime Minister offered to open the conference. At that time the Tamil Tiger terrorists had already detonated a bomb next to the car of the Admiral in charge of the Navy – first chairman of the Sri Lanka Branch of the Institute. All that was found of his bulletproof Mercedes was a little bit of the engine block at the bottom of a deep hole in the road.

The Prime Minister arrived amid tight security, and as host I ushered him into the auditorium.

At the start of proceedings some lovely ladies in diaphanous costumes were doing a "mermaid dance" to entertain us. The PM leaned over and whispered "I am not sure this will add to maritime safety – encouraging seafarers to look for mermaids when they should be looking out for other ships!"

When it came to the formal conference, he spoke for 15 minutes on maritime safety, coherent and well informed with no notes. The UK PM could not do that! I admired him.

6. Snowmen

In Britain, everyone knows how to make a snowman. You start by rolling three balls of snow. The biggest one becomes his bottom half. A slightly smaller one is placed on top to make his chest, and the smallest is placed on top of that as his head. A carrot for his nose, coal or pebbles

for eyes and buttons, a hat on his head, a scarf round his neck, a brush under his arm. Voila! Your snowman!

It was not until I was in charge of the Blue Funnel line Apprentices hostel in Liverpool, and one winter's day was making a snowman for our two young children, Katherine and David, that I realised that not everyone in the world knows how to make snowmen. The three of us were surrounded by an excited and attentive group of Malay cadets, who were commenting and taking photographs to send home. Not many snowmen in Malaya! We were pleased to pass on our expertise. I thought the British were good at something, but I was to learn otherwise.

In 1978, visiting friends Charles and Eugenia Koburger in Washington DC one January, I was about to get a surprise. In the North East of the USA, they had snowdrifts six or more feet deep and were dealing with it, with no problems at all. But in Washington, it is far enough south to miss most of the snow and it caused a few problems. Charles took me to visit a German-American family one evening and the path to their door was treacherously icy. We skirted round a statue of George Washington on the garden path and reached the front door. Our host welcomed us and asked me "What did you think of the snowman?" I

 said I had not seen it. All I had seen was what I took to be a marble statue of George Washington. He said his children had woken to see the garden covered in snow, and he suggested that they make a snowman.

They said "What is a snowman?" He had taken a dollar bill out of his pocket, pointed to the picture of George Washington on it and said "Make a snowman like that!" They had sculpted the statue from snow and ice.

I was amazed, and really quite upset. Although the children were American, in my mind I was recalling the scores for football matches. The score for making snowmen was about "Germany 10 England 2."

7. Norwegian Nerds

Whilst teaching at Trondheim Technical University in Norway, I stayed at an Esso Motor Inn about half a mile from the college. I walked to and from the University past a farm, where I could see lots of cages full of furry animals. At coffee time one morning I asked my host, Professor Arnfinn Hammer, what the furry animals were.

He said "They are nerds!"

Me "There are no such animals as nerds!"

Him "Yes there are! Surely you know what nerds are?"

Impasse.

Trying to break the deadlock, I asked "What are they called in Norwegian?"

He said "Mink"

Me "They are called mink in English as well!"

Him "Ah! Sorry, they must be Nerds in German!" (German Nerz = Mink)

Professor Hammer had a German wife and sometimes forgot which language he was using.

We had several impasses in our conversations. We sorted out salmon and various other fish names. However, I still do not know the name of the huge animal that came towards him out of a snowy forest and gave him a fright (I tried Bear, Moose, Elk, Stag, a every other English name, but saw no glimmer of recognition).

8. Luxury Yacht Sales

A good friend of mine in Japan told me the story about one of his friends who did a lot of business in Abu Dhabi in the Arabian Gulf. He was very friendly with the sheikhs, one of whom showed him a painting of a luxury yacht moving through blue water in Venice. The sheikh asked "Could you get me one of those?" Always wishing to please, the Japanese businessman said "Yes!" He went back to Japan and commissioned a Naval Architect to design a luxury motor yacht, as nearly as possible the same as the one in the painting.

Pleased with his product, he returned to Abu Dhabi and showed the sheikh the plans. The sheikh was very disappointed. He said the plans were nothing like the painting, because they included the underwater hull of the boat, which you could not see on the painting. Having carefully and politely explained that you cannot have the top half of the boat without the lower hull, they proceeded to discuss the layout of the staterooms and deck areas and things became more harmonious. Eventually, they explored the foc'sle area where there we very small cabins for crew members. The sheikh said, "Crew members are lower class people, aren't they? I don't want them on my boat!" More polite explanations were called for.

Eventually all was agreed and the boat built and delivered. Unfortunately, at the launching/naming ceremony, a bigger and better yacht belonging to another Government Minister went past. More disappointment and a long misunderstanding when a member of the sheikh's staff refused to pay for it! Difficult people to do business with!

9. The Angles and the Saxons

Suffolk is part of East Anglia, settled in the Middle Ages by immigrant Angles from the mainland of Europe. Essex is the land of the East Saxons, a different tribe. They did not get on very well when they were on the continent and mutual suspicion still exists today, when they are all supposed to be English. An amazing 1,400 years of animosity! The dividing line is the River Stour, which is pronounced differently depending on whether you are 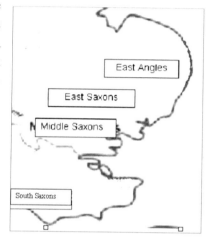 from Essex or Suffolk. One pronounces it "Stower", the other "Stooer." I admit I can never remember which is which, which is not very helpful.

One manifestation of this suspicion was told to me when I was inspecting courses at Felixstowe Docks in Suffolk. They asked me where I came from and I said "Essex!" At coffee time they told me the story of Suffolk parents with a teenage daughter. Like most teenage daughters she was difficult to handle and kept staying out late at night with a boy. When invited to bring him home to meet her parents, she refused. They began to suspect that there must be something peculiar about him. Was he too old for her?

Too young? Foreign? A Gipsy? Their imaginations ran wild. Eventually they made her tell them the reason for her shameful refusal to bring him home. Brimming with tears, she confessed – he was from Essex!

When the Nautical Institute was developing rapidly, an East Anglian Branch was formed, centred mainly around Ipswich in Suffolk and Colchester/Harwich in Essex. I often wonder why it failed?

10. Begging in London and in Towcester

While I was working full time, I had only one experience that involved the trials and tribulations of a street beggar. I was smartly dressed, walking down Southampton Row in London, on my way to a meeting, when I realised one of my shoelaces was undone. The pavement was very busy, so I chose a quiet and wide section upon which to crouch down and retie it. A peculiar thing then happened, half the people walking past looked at me with some embarrassment and compassion. The other half deliberately swerved away, turned their heads and ignored me as they walked past. It was not until I stood up that I realised I had been crouching beside a notice, written on card, which said "Please give generously, wife and children to support!" The space had previously been occupied by a beggar.

Since joining the ranks of the (almost) retired, I have had more experience of street collecting. In London, the Honourable Company of Master Mariners acted as a collecting centre for King George's Fund for Sailors.

Collecting from city bankers and office workers at railway stations was a bit soul destroying. A few people came up to us and said they had family members who had been at sea, and gave generously, but most clung to their wallets as they walked past. I never filled my collecting tin. Our most successful collector was Mrs Etain Barrett, wife of a senior member of the Honourable Company. She collected in a narrow alleyway in the Inns of Court, near the Headquarters ship "Wellington". The lawyers were no more generous than the bankers but Etain told them a compelling story about the good cause, whilst blocking their pathway. Her tin was always full to the top. On one occasion she told us of a lawyer who refused bluntly to donate. She told her story about the good works, but he still refused. Eventually Etain asked "Why won't you support us?" He replied, somewhat angrily "Look Woman! When I came the other way, I gave you £5, I am not going to give you any more!" Etain apologised and let him pass.

Street collecting with the Towcester and District Lions Club is much easier. Here, most people are much more friendly and generous. My best period of collecting was on a summer's day, outside the Post Office in Market Square. The shepherdess who looks after the sheep on the racecourse approached me with her border collie sheepdog. She asked if I would look after the dog while she queued in the Post Office (it could be a long job). All the time I had the

158

dog with me, everyone came to see the dog and gave very generously. Human psychology is a strange thing. Why should a dog make people more generous?

11. The Romans

The Empire

Commodore Ibrahim Hussein from Egypt sat next to me as I drove us through the Cheshire countryside on our way to visit an electronics company in the Midlands. The road was straight for miles and miles. I said to him "One of the advantages of having the Romans invade Britain is that they left us with some straight roads. This is one of them – Watling Street"

He seemed surprised "Romans?" he said "What a coincidence - we had them in my country too! So they came all the way to Britain as well?" When you think about it, the Romans had a huge empire. They actually united most of Europe in the same way that the European Union is trying to do today. It is a pity it all fell apart – I think corruption and nepotism had something to do with it.

The Car Park

Walking with our children round the walls of the City of Chester on a summer day, we met a fully dressed Roman centurion coming the other way. He looked very smart and the children were very interested and impressed. There must have been a re-enactment taking place somewhere among the Roman ruins. Whenever we visited castles or other historic places and buildings we always tried to teach the children a bit of history relevant to the site. Visiting one fortification in North Wales, I was talking about a battle which had taken place in Roman times and one of the youngest children, getting enthusiastic, said "Do you think they parked their chariots in the car park where we left our car?" I was not sure of the answer to that one. The trouble with history teachers is that their lessons always fall short on the details.

More Home and Family

1. Earning Your Living

We often hear the expression "money does not grow on trees" and it is important that children learn that they will be expected to earn a living when they grow up. Usually the parents explain this to their children, but in our case, the children worked it out for themselves.

"We know where the money comes from, for us to buy food and clothes"

Me: "Where does it come from?"

"It comes from the Polytechnic!"

Me: "That's right"

"You are a teacher and at the end of each lesson, you take a plate round the class and the students put money in!"

Me: "That is nearly right, but not quite"

The children had learned from Sunday School about collections at the end of a lesson and had put two and two together.

I explained that the Polytechnic pays money into our bank account. I did not explain that while Derek Hatton and Mrs Thatcher were at political daggers drawn, the Polytechnic might not pay the money. When you go to the bank and there may not be any salary there, it makes you more appreciative of the times when it is.

I thought a lot about the children's simple idea of rewarding teachers at the end of a lesson. I can think of one staff member who might have been a better teacher if we had implemented the collecting-plate system, but I was not allowed to do that!

2. Leighton Buzzard

In 1963, our bridesmaid, Iona ("Nonie") MacKinnon was teaching Physical Education in Leighton Buzzard and we went in our Ford Popular to visit her with our two children, Katherine and David. Anyone who has children will realise that the car gets full of toys, and anyone who has owned an old Ford Popular, will know that it had a strange transverse springing arrangement at the back, which meant it swayed a lot on corners.

We put the children to bed and Ann stayed with them, while I was to take Nonie back to her "digs". It was a very dark night. We drove off in silence, but as we turned the first sharp corner, there was an almighty din - a whoosh and tinkling sound - from the parcel shelf at the back. Nonie was startled and said "What on earth was that?" I explained very calmly "Don't worry, it is a mouse running up and down the back shelf, playing a xylophone!" She was even more startled, until I explained that it was a pull-along toy.

3. Sunday Afternoon Walks

In the early 1970s, when our five children were not yet in their teens, the family would go for walks after Sunday lunch. There were plenty of pleasant country walks on the Wirral, the Wirral Way, Thurstaston Hill, the Dales, Royden Park with its Model Steam Railway etc. Sometimes their friends joined us and, of course we took Lassie, the dog. We ALL enjoyed the fresh air and exercise, or so we thought...

One Parents Open Day at Pensby Infants School, Ann and I visited Peter's classroom. As the parents entered, the children were ushered out to play games. We noticed that before he left Peter, who must have been about six, hid one of his books under all the others in his desk. When it came to inspecting his work, we dug out the book to see what he wanted to hide. Each week, all the children were encouraged to complete a "news" book saying what they had done on holiday and at home. Peter had written "On Sunday, we went for a walk on the Wirral Way, we saw two lions and a tiger!"

When Peter arrived home we said, "Why did you say things in your news book which were not true? We did not see lions and tigers on Sunday, did we?" Peter's reply said it all: "I know we didn't, but the truth is so BORING!"

4. Chastisement and the Glass Museum

I rather like the idea of children being sent to "The Naughty Stair" when they have misbehaved. A bit of quiet contemplation and being excluded from the action often changes their attitude. It seems to work for some of the grandchildren when used by their parents.

Ann and I came across a different way of influencing the behaviour of our five. We came across it by chance. I had been looking for somewhere to take the family on a wet Saturday and came across an article about the glass museum in St Helens. It sounded interesting, so I suggested to the family: "Shall we go to Pilkington's Glass Museum!" There was a 100 per cent vociferous vote "NO"– other than from Ann and I who would quite like to have gone.

From that time on we had a new weapon. Any time the children did not want to do something we said "If you don't want to do that, we will take you to Pilkington's Glass Museum!" It worked a treat – instant compliance! When the children left home Ann and I went to the museum. It is fascinating. The children did not know what they were missing.

A Really Special Place to Visit

I was going down in the lift at the Polytechnic one spring when I overheard two of the cleaners discussing their summer holiday plans:

"Where are you going for your holidays this year, Mary?"

"A hotel on the Costa Brava again, I suppose, it gets so boring – same old Spain every time!"

I was a senior lecturer and Ann and I could not afford to take our young family to hotels in Spain. The best we managed was tented campsites in Wales. One year we were so poor we could not even afford that. We got the children round the table and said "We cannot afford to go away on holiday this year, but you can each choose your favourite place for a day out, and whatever you choose, we promise to take you!" Katherine, David, Nicholas and Alison never had any problem choosing, but Peter did. He thought and thought for ages. "Come on Peter!" we said

"Where would you really really like to go. Don't worry about the money – if you choose it, we promise to take you there!" After a lot more thought Peter said "I would really like a day out at the Council rubbish tip at Thurstaston!" Peter had his day out and collected a lot of old broken radios and electronic equipment, from which he built a control centre in his bedroom and supplied music etc to the other children's bedrooms at quite a reasonable rental charge. A budding environmentalist and entrepreneur!

5. A Very Old Mersey Ferry

The draft marks at the bow and stern of ships are normally six inches high. The bottom of the number, for example 6, shows 6 feet draft, the top is 6 feet 6 inches. Some ships use roman numerals because they have a line top and bottom and that makes the reading easier.

In the 1960s, standing with a very young Katherine on the landing stage at Liverpool Pierhead, looking at the Mersey ferry "Royal Iris", she looked at the bow:
Katherine: "Dad, That is a very old ship!" (It was quite old.)
Me: "What makes you think that?"
Katherine: "The numbers are in Roman numerals"

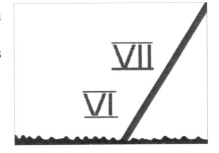

6. Artistic Talents

Bottom of the class

When God was handing out artistic talents, I think I must have been absent. In my first two years at Grammar School in Horsham, out of a class of 31, my position in the art examinations hovered between 28th and 31st, with one exception. On that occasion, I had picked up the exam paper, and when I read it, my heart sank – we were asked to paint a picture entitled "A Bus Stop". It was to test our ability to draw people as they queued for the bus. I could not draw people, but as a country boy, I was quite good at drawing cows. So I drew a country lane, with a bus stop. It was a quiet lane and nobody was waiting for the bus. There was only one person in the picture – a farm hand walking behind the cow as it passed the stop. The cow took up most of the picture. The Art Master said "Not what I expected!" But I came 7th! Next term I was back to 29th.

Another School: Another Try

At the age of 12 we moved to Dovercourt, Essex and I joined the 3rd Form at Harwich County High School. Still 31st in the class but this time 21 girls and only 10 boys. The art teacher was Kathleen ("Katy") Green. I had similar results until we were introduced to ceramics. We had to model a figure sitting on a seat. I was still not very good at figures and spent very little time on the person. Instead of a park bench or seat, I modelled a tree stump. I was good at tree stumps and very proud of my efforts. Praise from the teacher and an invitation to put it in the cupboard, after which it would be fired and I could paint it. Queuing for the cupboard, I was pushed in the back and the clay finished as a crumpled mess. End of my efforts in art!

Katherine's Homework

Katherine, our eldest, inherited my lack of ability in the art department. When asked to draw or paint a picture for homework, she would struggle for ages to illustrate the subject. She would add more and more paint and it would look less and less like the subject it was supposed to be. On other occasions, Ann and I would add a bit more paint, but that did not help. Katherine remembers one very wet masterpiece that had to be finished off with a hair dryer. On one occasion she crumpled up her efforts in despair, and I had to iron it to make it ready for handing in.

Eventually all the family did Katherine's homework. It added interest at the tea table when she came home from school, a chorus would ask "What mark did WE get for art this week?"

David's Competition Entry

Katherine had spent a long time during the week preparing her entry for a children's art competition in the church hall in Heswall village. David was busy with homework during the week, but we reminded him on Saturday morning that there was going to be a painting competition that morning. He picked up a brush and applied it with a few

168

strokes to create the image of a sailing ship. He won first prize! Life is so unfair! His train pictures are good too!

The Old Folks Home

In her late 80s my mother had dementia and was persuaded to go into Alexandra House, a Methodist home looking over the entrance to Harwich Harbour. The staff were very nice and encouraged the old people to take an interest in things. Visiting, Ann and I saw very nice watercolour paintings of wild flowers on display with the initials "MH" on them. They were by my mother, still showing a talent even when her mind was so confused. Perhaps that is where David got his talents.

The Next Generation

The grandchildren have been fortunate to have access to ceramics classes and other facilities where caring and talented teachers help them to produce very creditable efforts which grace the shelves of our home, starting with painting of ready-moulded pieces and moving on from there. The pretty coloured seahorses are a present from our granddaughter Amy Mead.

7. Bedrooms and Beds

Having five children made the allocation of beds and bedrooms an important affair. There was sometimes competition and Peter wanted to get in ahead of the rest. His grandmother lived with us in a large bed-sitting room and was surprised – and fortunately mildly amused - when Peter went in to see her and asked "Grandma, when you die, can I have your room?"

Many years earlier in the mid 1960s, when it was time for everyone to "move up one" from the decorated basket in which the children started their lives, to a cot, to a single bed or bunk bed, it was Katherine, as the eldest, who needed a new bed. I was an Assistant Lecturer on a very meagre salary (I started lecturing on £1,100 a year). We could not afford a new bed, so I was despatched to read all the postcard advertisements in newsagents' windows, to find her a good-quality second-hand single bed.

The first newsagent's window had no beds, but it advertised an interesting sailing dinghy. I sighed, forgot about it, and went miles and miles to every newsagent I knew – no  beds! I was drawn back to the first window and the boat. I thought there was no harm in going to look at the boat; I might like to buy one in the future. When I saw the boat, a 10-foot Yachting World "Heron", it was in good condition, but I also learned that there was a road trailer and an outboard motor included in the price. I could not resist! Arriving home with my purchase, I was not popular with Ann (or with Katherine – who slept on a spare mattress on the floor for the next three months).

The official launching of our "new" boat took place at Chester on the River Dee. Ann stayed ashore with the young ones. With Katherine and David, I set out into mid-stream and only just made it to the other bank before the boat sank. It had been out of the water a long time, the wood had dried out and it took a few hours of soaking to regain its water-tightness. Ann told us she watched as the boat went lower and lower in the water and was quite relieved when we all leapt out in the shallows by the other bank.

8. Bombs and Terrorists

Liverpool Dental Hospital
Daughter Katherine, in her early teens, was having a difficult and painful operation at Liverpool Dental Hospital. The dental surgeon was drilling down into the root of an infected "dead" tooth right at the front of her mouth. Suddenly all the alarms went off and we were all rushed out into the car park. It was a freezing cold day. It could not have happened at a worse time. There were no flames or smoke coming from the building. I would have been very angry if it had just been a drill. It wasn't. These were the days of IRA bombers in England and it was a bomb alert.

Eventually, the "all clear" was given and we went back for the operation to be completed. The full story emerged later. A student at the University School of Dentistry had got up late that morning (with a hangover, I suspect). He had rushed into the building late, dumped his bag in the hallway and scurried off to his lecture. Someone who saw him thought he might be a terrorist, and raised the alarm. Why are some university students so irresponsible and thoughtless??

Delhi Airport
After a long flight from London, the passengers bound for Bombay were keen to get the Delhi passengers off the plane and continue to their destination. A security team boarded the plane and were carrying out long drawn out procedures. Everyone was tired and irritable and complaining, except one Indian gentleman who stood next to me calmly and quietly waiting. I asked him if he shared our impatience. He said "Not at all. I was on the plane highjacked to Damascus by Leila Khaled in 1969. I was lucky to have been a captive on the plane for a very short time. I was one of the first to be released. I never complain about security procedures – they can take as long as they like if it stops me going through that experience again!" Whenever I get fed up with airport security, I think of his words!

9. Really Somebody

Ann had been a soprano with Wirral Choral Society for several years before I was persuaded to supplement the basses in a Christmas concert and finished up singing with them for more than 16 years. We had a young teenage

 soprano, Jackie Denin, who was a real asset to the choir and, her father Ken, like me, was persuaded to become one of the basses.

A few months later, meeting Ken in his greengrocery shop in Heswall he said:

"Until I joined the choir, I was a nobody, but now I feel I am a really somebody!"

He went on to explain that he had come home to his family one choir night and announced this step-up in his life.

"I really feel somebody in the choir"

The choir mistress said:

"Somebody is flat"

"Somebody comes in at all the wrong places"

"So now I know I am SOMEBODY!"

10. Texting

Some young people – and indeed some not so young – can do mobile phone texting at an amazing speed. Our daughter-in-law Gaynor amazes us by replying to text messages instantly. We almost thought that she was writing the answers before we had asked the questions. But no, she is just very fast!

I read in a magazine article that young people were using their thumbs so much for texting that their thumbs were growing larger. Discussing this with granddaughter

Sandra, I said that I thought this was unlikely. In order to prove my point, I said "That is nonsense! I do all my typing with the index finger of my left hand and that is still the same size as my right index finger." To prove it, I showed the two fingers together. The left one was significantly bigger and longer. I lost the argument.

11. Admiring David Tennant

Our younger daughter Alison thinks the actor David Tenant is wonderful and never misses a chance to go and see him. He was recording the radio programme "Chain Reaction" with Richard Wilson at Broadcasting House in London and she invited Ann and I to join her at the recording.

The tickets are free, but the BBC always wants the auditorium full, so they issue far more tickets than there are seats and you have to queue. Alison told us that David Tennant was so popular that we must arrive very early and queue for a long time to be sure of getting in. As we turned into Portland Place my heart sank a bit, as there were queues all the way up to Weymouth Street and round the block into Hallam Street and beyond. We thought "We did not know he was THAT popular!"

We parked the car and sought out the end of the queue. We had expected there to be a lot of young girls, but there was a whole mixture of ages, including a lot of men in their

30s and 40s. Strange. Just to be sure we asked "Are you queuing for the David Tennant radio show?" It is just as well we asked. They replied "No! We are going to vote in the Polish Elections at the Embassy in Portland Place!"

The real David Tennant queue was quite short and because Ann and Alison both have "dicky" hips, they kindly let us sit in the foyer. The show was very good – worth waiting for.

12. Bletchley Park

NOTE: I was in trouble when I wrote my first book of stories, because it did not have a nice picture of granddaughter Amy, in it. Here is a nice picture of Amy, now aged 10. Having done this duty, Amy will now let me tell the following story!

Many primary schools teach history in an imaginative and interesting way, involving families with their memorabilia of important events, like World War II. Our

family has a collection of gas masks, ration books, clothes coupons, identity cards, Government leaflets and posters etc, which can help the teachers bring "recent" history to life for the children. We are also lucky to live near Bletchley Park, home of the Code Breakers, who broke the German Enigma codes in World War II, and thereby shortened the war by about two years and saved thousands of lives. It has excellent displays, and I took

Amy (aged 9) and Daniel (aged 12) to see them on a wet winter afternoon.

The volunteers who man the exhibitions are nice friendly people and when I explained that Amy was doing World War II at school this term, she said "You should visit the WWII exhibition upstairs, the Post Office, the motor garage, the naval exhibits and the special Winston Churchill exhibition."

Some of the exhibits reminded me of 1939 – 1945, and I was able to tell the children that my mother washed things by hand and put them through a mangle, we saw an old Vauxhall 12 car just like the one my father drove, and pictures and models of ships like HMS "Duke of York" which I had visited in Portsmouth as a young schoolboy. I had lived in the country where we had a coal-fire range and oil lamps, so the electric irons and gas stoves were too modern for my "war".

As we walked back to reception, to return our electronic "guides", I realised we had not visited the Winston Churchill section. I thought there might be no need, as Amy probably knew about him.

Me: "Amy, who was our Prime Minister in the War?"

Amy: "Adolph Hitler"

Kindly lady behind the reception desk "Nearly right, Amy, Adolph Hitler wanted to be our Prime Minister, but he never made it!"

I am willing to bet that Amy will never forget it was Winston Churchill.

13. Hospital Visits

People who are in hospital after an operation develop what is called a "Daily Mirror mind". They cannot cope with the heavy stuff like the Times or the Daily Telegraph, they like short simple stories –and a few pictures if possible.

Eric Knowles, one of my colleagues on the Mersey Mission to Seafarers Committee, went into Arrowe Park hospital in Birkenhead for quite a serious operation. At this time, Ann and I were subscribers to "Readers Digest" and the latest edition arrived on our doormat just as I was going to visit. When we were at sea, reading materials were often scarce and some Readers Digests were read over and over again. They were popular. Ideal for Eric, I thought.

When he recovered he came back to the Mission Committee and thanked everyone for their good wishes and visits. He said "I was particularly grateful to the chairman, who, when I was at my lowest ebb brought in a copy of Readers Digest with a leading article on euthanasia." I should have checked the contents before giving it to him!

Although Eric was very ill, during my first visit, he asked for quiet because the chap in the next bed was really ill and not likely to survive the night. Next day the bed was empty. I said "Did he die?" Eric said "No! The hospital has just introduced a new microwave cook-on-the-ward meal system. There are a few teething problems. My neighbour felt a bit better today, but his food was cold, so he has gone to complain!"

14. Listening and Hearing

As we get older, our ears become less sensitive to high notes. It is a gradual process. In Pensby Road, Heswall, we lived next to Mr Lascelles, who was a former physics teacher. He was a radio "ham" and talked to people all over the world. His son was also a scientist interested in radio frequencies. He was personal assistant to Sir Bernard Lovell at Jodrell Bank Radio Telescope / Observatory. Mr Lascelles Senior understood radio frequencies and sound frequencies. He measured the change in his hearing over the years, and he and I compared notes. Incidentally, when he was in the RAF during the war, he discovered that if you wrote neatly on a classroom blackboard, everyone believed what you wrote. When I started teaching, I tried to write neatly!

My next encounter with ear problems was at Arrowe Park Hospital on the Wirral. For several years Ann had complained that I did not hear what she said, so I was despatched for tests. The verdict: my hearing was perfectly normal for a man of my age. The consultant said "I think the reason you don't hear your wife, is that you are not listening!" He may have had a point.

A few more years went by, and we had moved to Towcester. Same problem, same solution. I was despatched to

178

Northampton General Hospital for more hearing tests. They told me I had lost a bit more of the sensitivity to high notes. At Towcester Choral that evening the basses asked how the test had gone. I told them: "The specialist says my ears are quite normal, but unless I get hearing aids, I would be able to hear men clearly, but not hear the higher voices of women and children". To a man, in chorus, the basses said: "You lucky so and so, we wish we could get some of that!"

15. Belle Baulk Park

In recent years, our son Nick has lived with us while recovering from a series of operations. Unable to work or travel, he has made wonderful use of the local environment, helping to set up a local branch of the Wildlife Trust and producing beautiful photographs of local wild birds and animals, which are sold as calendars and cards in aid of the charity.

The parkland and floodplain near our house has been named "Belle Baulk Park" and Nick organised a questionnaire to ask our neighbours how they would like to see it used. Community activities are often greeted with a shrug, but wild life issues have a wonderful effect. The replies helped Nick to make presentations to the Town Council and Rotary Club and a "wildlife friendly" area has now been established along the River Tove. One request proved difficult. When asked what sort of wildlife she would like to see, one young lady, named Sky, a neighbour's daughter of under 5, said she wanted lions and kangaroos. When she helped with "litter picking" in the park, Nick gave her what she asked for – not real, but fluffy varieties.

During a session clearing aggressive Canadian pondweed from the lake, two girls in their early teens asked if they could help. Dragging a very heavy metal rake across the pond needed tough adults; so Nick asked them to go round and collect the plastic bags and bottles that accumulate in the area. Whilst they were doing this, a plastic bag blew into a high bush and the girls climbed up to get it. The climb proved to be fun, and they were in the bush as a lady walked past and chastised them for damaging plants. When the girls returned with their haul of rubbish, they told Nick about the incident: "What a strange woman! Didn't she realise we were saving the planet!"

16. Booking for The Theatre

There were two main theatres in Liverpool, the Royal Court and the Playhouse. We were staying in Heswall with friends Alan and Margery Denham and decided a trip to the theatre in Liverpool was a good idea. We liked the look of the very light comedy at the Royal Court and I was asked to book the tickets while in town. I knew the two theatres well and went to the box office and bought four tickets for the front row of the circle. As I led the party into the theatre that evening, a chorus behind me said "This isn't the Royal Court, it is the Playhouse!" Well, they are very near to one another.

We took our coats off and settled into our seats in the Circle, not really looking forward to a serious avant-garde drama. A very large and officious usherette came to the end of our row and said - almost shouted - an unusual request: "DO YOU MIND TAKING YOUR COATS OFF." We told her that we had already taken them off. That made her really mad. "THAT'S NOT WHAT I MEANT! TAKE THEM OFF THE BALCONY RAIL!!" We obliged and sat, chastised, waiting for the play. It was the play by N. F. Simpson, The One Way Pendulum, where the man goes up to the mantle-piece, picks up the skull and shakes it. His wife says, "Why did you do that?" and he says, "It is not working; it does not remind me of death". Not quite the comedy we were looking forward to!!

In happier times, standing in the queue at the Theatre Box Office in New Brighton with the children, David, then about six or seven, said "What is an oap?" A little old lady behind us said "I am an oap!" David had seen the seat prices were reduced for children and oaps. Ann and I are now Old Aged Pensioners and are enjoying the concessions for oaps.

Booking by telephone for the Somerset Maugham play "The Circle" at Milton Keynes Theatre, I had a very intimate conversation about the receptionist's husband's inside leg measurement. The conversation went something like this:

Me: "Have you two seats for tonight's performance?"

She lists seats of various numbers, prices and places.

Me (to narrow the options a bit): "Have you a seat with plenty of leg room as my knees ache if I cannot stretch them."

Her: "I know just what you mean. My husband has an inside leg measurement of 37.5 inches and we always try to get a seat near the aisle for him. Personally, I suffer from the opposite problem; I am so short my feet don't reach the floor. We went for a pre-theatre drink recently. The seats were very high – just right for him, but so high he had to lift me up. I felt like a little girl!" Most London theatres wouldn't have had time for such a nice chat.

Anyway, she found us excellent seats and it was a very good play. Susan Hampshire playing the older woman in a play in which she starred as the young one twenty years ago.

17. Read Label Before Use

Preparing for a trip to the coast, early morning, leaving the bathroom. Most of my toiletries already packed, including deodorant. Glance in the drawer, no need to unpack deodorant, I see a spare spray with a red top. Shake it vigorously and apply generous under arms. Feel as if I am on fire and cry for help. Ann administers soothing cream. Then read the label "Deep Heat" Mentholatum Muscle Spray. Moral "Read the label first".

On an earlier occasion I had had an itch in a private place. In the dark I felt for the tube of soothing cream and applied it. Wrong cream. "Deep Heat " again! When will I learn?

18. My Haircut and Millionaires

Last year the girl who cuts my hair must have thought I needed a new image. She cut my hair with a tatty fringe, and when I looked into the mirror I thought I looked like the millionaire Formula One Racing Tycoon Bernie Ecclestone.

As he seems to attract money and gorgeous girls, I thought this might change my life. It didn't, so I have gone back to my old hairstyle again, but grown a beard so I can look like Alan Sugar.

It sometimes makes me a bit grumpy but it has not made me rich!

19. Manoeuvres in the Dark

At 7.45 pm on an autumn evening, walking along the dark pathway from our house to a meeting of Towcester Lions Club, I heard youths shouting. I thought "Vandals! Up to no good!" But no, as I got closer, I realised they were shouting "One!" "Two!" "Three!" etc. The noise was coming from a pitch-dark parade ground near the Army Cadets' headquarters. I walked past, and came to the main road, where a smartly dressed Army Cadet was anxiously looking up the road.

Me "Have the lights failed on the parade ground?"
Him "No sir! There are no lights on the parade ground"
Me "Do you normally parade in the dark?"
Him "No sir! At this time of year we meet earlier and parade while it is still light"
I must have looked puzzled.
He added "This week we are being inspected by a visiting senior officer who told us he would inspect us promptly at 8 p.m.!"
I wished I could have stayed to watch the inspection of manoeuvres in the dark, but I had a meeting to go to…

20. Dan in Church

Before Daniel was at school, Alison took him to church one Sunday.
In the middle of the service, Dan told the Vicar: "Jesus died a long time ago!" She was pleased and said "Yes, Dan, he died and came back, and is with us now!"
Dan said: "I see, he died, went away for a bit, and then came back!"
She asked Dan if his Mummy taught him about Jesus.
"No!" he said "I just knew it!"

21. Train Announcements

A couple of inches of snow in October might be expected to disrupt transport, but the roads seemed to cope all right. The London train was late arriving at Milton Keynes and the conductress/guard apologised for the delay caused by signals at Rugby. When we arrived in Bletchley, she repeated the apology and added "The delay was made worse at Milton Keynes because there was nobody to help get a disabled passenger on board." I am not sure how that made the passenger feel. At Leighton Buzzard she said "I would like to welcome all the passengers who joined here, and apologise to half of them who had the doors slammed in their faces. If I had known their train had been cancelled, I would not have done that!" At Tring she added to the list "I don't believe this, problems with signals here as well" She was sounding more and more depressed. In a tired fed-up voice "Ladies and Gentlemen, we are approaching Berkhampstead....Oops, as you know, we do not stop here!" As we arrived in London the list of delays was repeated. She made all the passengers smile, but would probably need counselling herself.

I could not help thinking of the West Indian Guard on the Liverpool Virgin trains who used to start his announcements, by saying in a very cheery voice "Is everybody happy?" I am not sure you can teach that in a politically correct railway charm school. Pity!

Reading Between the Lines

A group of passengers were standing on Milton Keynes station waiting for the London train. I looked at the display it said "0921 Train on time" but also said "Delayed by an incident on preceding train." I turned to my neighbour and said I found it confusing. He replied that he had travelled on the line a long time and was no longer confused. "I always choose the worst option" he said "To me, that simply says 'Delayed'!"

22. Blessed by the Bishop

Since moving to Northamptonshire, Ann, daughter Alison and I have been singing in two local choirs. The Orphean Singers in the village of Hanslope were the first choir we joined. About forty people sing for the joy of singing, but most of the concerts are given in aid of charities, so the benefits are threefold – we enjoy it, the audience enjoys it, and the charity benefits from the income.

In many of the villages in Northamptonshire, there were beautiful old churches which were not being used very much, other than for occasional Sunday services, often with one vicar serving three or four parishes. It does not take much imagination to realise that these under-utilised buildings could become centres for other community activities, plays, concerts, children's' groups etc. Most of the churches needed to install toilets if they were to become real community centres. So for several years, the Orphean singers sang in villages all around the area, to supplement their "Toilet Funds".

St Nicholas's Church is a landmark in Harwich and appears in the background of this 1843 painting of the fast paddle steamer "Orwell" which plied between Ipswich and London.

Visiting Harwich in search of Ann's family history, we were welcomed by two charming elderly ladies as we entered St Nicholas's Church. They were helpful with our research and remembered some of Ann's family. We told them about all the beautiful village churches in Northamptonshire, and why we had visited them. They listened politely, then told us that St Nicholas's had had a "Toilet Fund" as part of recent refurbishment, and they proudly said that their toilet was very special. One lady said, "When the Bishop came to open the refurbished church, I was the one who had to escort him to the new toilet, while he blessed it!" We could not beat that!

Also available from Len Holder:

A Light-Hearted
Look at Seafaring
and other
stories

Len
Holder

A Light-Hearted Look at Seafaring
and other stories

ISBN: 9781906205171, 200pp

£10.00

At the age of 72, Len Holder was persuaded to write some of his
observations down. The stories include schooldays in Harwich, sailing and
sea scouting, serving with Alfred Holt and Company's Blue Funnel and
Glen Lines, joining the Honorable and lecturing at Liverpool Polytechnic,
living on the Wirral and traveling worldwide as a consultant. The proceeds
from the sale of this book will be donated to maritime and medical
charities.